DATA BANK ON CURRENT AFFAIRS AND MISCELLANEOUS G.K.

AF519886

DATA BANK
ON
CURRENT AFFAIRS
AND
MISCELLANEOUS G.K.

Compiled and Edited by

Arvind M. Dwivedi

ANMOL PUBLICATIONS PVT. LTD.

NEW DELHI - 110 002 (INDIA)

ANMOL PUBLICATIONS PVT. LTD.
4374/4B, Ansari Road, Daryaganj
New Delhi-110 002
www.anmolbooks.com

Data Bank on Current Affairs and Miscellaneous G.K.
© Reserved
First Edition 2002
ISBN 81-261-1007-4

[Responsibility for the facts stated, opinions expressed, conclusions reached and plagiarism, if any, in this volume is entirely that of the Editor. The Publishers bear no responsibility for them, whatsoever.]

PRINTED IN INDIA

Published by J. L. Kumar for Anmol Publications Pvt. Ltd., New Delhi-110 002 and Printed at Tarun Offset Press, Delhi.

CONTENTS

PREFACE

The present age is the age of competitions. Gone are the days when the degrees were enough to get a job. Now the thorough study of any subject is required to get through in any competitive examination. The objective multiple choice type questions are asked almost in all the competitions. In order to meet the increasing demand of the aspirants, we have prepared the Data Bank on Current Affairs and Miscellaneous G.K. and feel pleasure on presenting the same before you. It is concise, comprehensive and dependable which has a wide coverage of the syllabus.

The proportion of questions from Current affairs and miscellaneous G.K. in General study has get tremendous increase in the recent past. Near about 15% questions are asked from this portion. In the present data bank we have touched all the corners of syllabus as well as the latest pattern of questions asked in UPSC, SSC, LIC, GIC, CDS, NDA and other examinations. We have taken utmost care in preparing the questions with particular gradation and level of the various examination.

We shall feel grateful to the readers if they send us their valuable comments so that further improvements may be made in the subsequent editions of the book.

—Arvind M. Dwivedi

CURRENT AFFAIRS

1 28th Olympic Games will be held in:
(a) Toronto (b) Athens
(c) Tokyo (d) Atlanta

2 Asia's biggest Auto Expo held on 12 jan. 2001 in:
(a) Mumbai (b) Chennai
(c) Hyderabad (d) Delhi

3 On 23rd Jan. 2001 'The best poet' Videocon Award was given to:
(a) Shank Ghosh (b) Narendra Mohan
(c) Atal Behari Bajpayee (d) Harivansh Rai Bachchan

4 The 87th Science Conference (3-7 Jan. 2001) was held in:
(a) Chandigarh (b) Delhi
(c) Bangalore (d) Pune

5 On 24th Dec. 1999, 6 Muslim terrorists hijacked an Indian Airlines Aeroplane, the aeroplane was:
(a) Airbus 387 (b) A - 387
(c) Boing 814/37 (d) IC 814

6 The Arjuna award 2000 was given to:
(a) Sunita Rai (b) P. Gopichand
(c) Sachin Tendulkar (d) Jagjit

7 The Dronacharya award 2000 was given to:
(a) Cannatha Annbosen (b) Captain Hawa Singh
(c) Ajay Sirohi (d) All the bove

8 DWR - 185 is a:
(a) Latest PC
(b) Latest quality of rice
(c) Latest quality of wheat
(d) Latest quality of submarine

9 What is T3A ?
(a) Latest tank made by Russia
(b) Latest fighter aircraft made by Russia
(c) World's fastest computer
(d) Submarine made by Russia

10 The size of the Rajasthan's annual 2000 - 2001 has been fixed at:
(a) Rs. 3412 crore

(b) Rs. 4146 crore
(c) Rs. 4800 crore
(d) Rs. 5000 crore

11 Who among the following won the Women's Hockey Test series held in April 2000?
(a) South Korea (b) Australia
(c) India (d) Germany

12 Which language is spoken by the majority of the people in Lakshadweep?
(a) Kannada (b) Malayalam
(c) Tamil (d) Telugu

13 In the terms of Indian Rupee, the exchange rate is the highest for:
(a) Riyal (b) British Pound
(c) US Dollar (d) Dinar

14 Name of the Indian bank having largest number of branches abroad:
(a) Bank of India (b) Indian Overseas Bank
(c) State Bank of India (d) Central Bank of India

15 Which Grand Slam event in tennis is held in the first month of every year?
(a) US Open (b) Wimbledon
(c) French Open (d) Australian Open

16 Name the country which will host the next Commonwealth Games:
(a) Mauritius
(b) Malaysia
(c) Sri Lanka
(d) India

17 In which district in the State of Bihar the worst ever massacre was done by a private army on Decmber 1, 1997 ?
(a) Jehanabad (b) Patna
(c) Aurangabad (d) Gaya

18 Name the place where the first World Sikh University has been set up recently:
(a) London (b) New York
(c) Sydney (d) Chicago

19 Who is the present Governor of the Reserve Bank of India?

(a) Prof. Madhu Dandwate (b) Montek Singh Ahluwalia
(c) C. Rangarajan (d) Dr. Bimal Jalan

20 Which of the two countries are the largest Uranium producers in the world?
(a) Italy and Spain (b) Peru and Russia
(c) USA and Russia (d) USA and Canada

21 Who among the following is the present president of USA?
(a) George W. Bush (b) Jimmy Carter
(c) Bill Clinton (d) Ronald Reagon

22 Who among the following is the present chairman of ISRO ?
(a) R. Chidambaram (b) A. P. J. Abdul Kalam
(c) Prof. K. Kasturirangan (d) Prof. Satish Dhawan

23 Who wrote the General theory of Employment, interest and Money?
(a) Kaldor (b) Marx
(c) Keynes (d) Marshall

24 Who among the following was the founder of Atomic theory?
(a) Benjamin Franklin (b) Madame Curie
(c) Albert Einstein (d) John Dalton

25 In which country, the next World Cup Cricket Tournament will be held?
(a) West Indies (b) India
(c) Australia (d) England

26 Which of the following countries recently launched a new range of ballistic missile called the 'Ghauri' ?
(a) China (b) Pakistan
(c) Russia (d) India

27 Recently Macau, a Portuguese colony was reverted to:
(a) China (b) Indonesia
(c) Japan (d) Thaieland

28 On January 4, 2000, India successfully launched maiden test flight of the indigenous Light Combat Aircraft from:
(a) Bangalore
(b) New Delhi
(c) Mumbai
(d) Hyderabad

29 Name the author of the 'Paradise Lost' ?

(a) Bharti Hari (b) Abul Fazal
(c) John Milton (d) Tulsidas

30 Which is the capital of Uttaranchal?
(a) Haridwar (b) Dehradun
(c) Nainital (d) Kosani

31 Russia celebrates 40 years of first flight of a human being into space. On this date 40 years ago Yuri Gagarin became the first person to enter space. This date is:
(a) 12 April (b) 11 January
(c) 11 April (d) 11 February

32 The 'Jamwde Oro' award the highest civilian honour of Spain is awarded to:
(a) Mahesh Bhupati (b) Gopi Chand
(c) Vishwanathan Anand (d) Leander Paes

33 Which star Cricketer has been awarded the prestigious 'Maharashtra Bhushan' award for the year 2000 - 01 ?
(a) Anil Kumble (b) Saurav Ganguly
(c) Sachin Tendulkar (d) Rahul Dravid

34 'Knight of the order of arts and letters' award by the French Government is given to:
(a) Arundhati Roy (b) Vikram Seth
(c) Khushwant Singh (d) None of these

35 'Saraswati Samman' is given to the person related to:
(a) Art (b) Music
(c) Poetry (d) Literature

36 President Laurent Kabila of Congo killed in a failed coup attempt on:
(a) 19th January, 2001 (b) 20th January, 2001
(c) 19th February, 2001 (d) 19th March, 2001

37 On 17th January, 2001 a surface to surface missile is successfully tested for the second time from a mobile launcher, its name is:
(a) Agni I (b) Agni III
(c) Agni II (d) Agni

38 The Chief Guest at the Republic Day Parade, 2001 was:
(a) Alik Likiaksa (b) Joseph Estrada
(c) Abdul Aziz Boutifilika (d) None of these

39 The recently elected Prime Minister of Israel is:
(a) Ariel Sharon (b) William Hewlett
(c) Arturo Vallarino (d) None of these

40 More than two crore people take holy dip in the Sangam on Mauni Amavasya, the holiest day of the Kumbha Mela held at Allahabad on:
(a) 26th February, 2001 (b) 26th January, 2001
(c) 26th December, 2001 (d) 26th November, 2001

41 The present Chief of Defence Staff is:
(a) Admiral Sushil Kumar
(b) General S. Padmanabhan
(c) Air Chief Anil Yashwant Tipnis
(d) None of these

42 The International Gandhi Peace Prize was given to:
(a) Mr. Nelson Mandela (b) V. N. Gadgil
(c) Fali Billimoria (d) None of these

43 Mr. Arun Netravali, who is known as India's Thomas Alva Edison is the president of:
(a) IBM (b) Infosys
(c) Bell Labs (d) Apple Computers

44 Who is the new Prime Minister of Japan?
(a) Mr. Li Peng (b) Mr. Alik Likiaksa
(c) Mr. Junichiro Kuizumi (d) None of these

45 The 16 BSF Soldiers were killed by Bangladesh rifles (BDR) on:
(a) April 9, 2001 (b) April 8, 2001
(c) April 7, 2001 (d) April 6, 2001

46 On which date the Lok Sabha approved the Union Budget:
(a) 24 April, 2001 (b) 25 April 2001
(c) 25 March, 2001 (d) 23 April, 2001

47 Name the Chief Minister of Jharkhand (Newly born state) ?
(a) Mr. Prabhat Kumar (b) Nityanand Swami
(c) Mr. Babulal Marandi (d) None of these

48 The UN Attorney General, Janet Reno upheld the decision giving custody of Elain Gonzalez to his father on January 13, 2000. The six year old Gonzalez had been staying with his relatives in Florida. Ellan Gonzalez holds the citizenship of:

(a) Miami (b) Pretoria
(c) Cuba (d) Ghana

49 Who is the new Chief Justice of Pakistan's Supreme Court?
(a) Justice Shahbuddin
(b) Justice Irshad Hussain Khan
(c) Justice Saiduzzeaman Siddique
(d) Justice Banimal Khan

50 Seamus Heaney won the £ 23 whitebred Book of the year award for his translation of the Anglo Saxon epic, Beowulf. He is the poet from:
(a) UK (b) USA
(c) Germany (d) Ireland

51 Who is the first Indian to head the Rotary Foundation, one of the richest bodies of the Rotary International?
(a) Kalyan Bannerjee (b) Sukhwinder Singh
(c) Ujjal Dosainjah (d) Bharat Kumar

52 Samjhauta Express runs between India and :
(a) Bangladesh (b) Pakistan
(c) Sri Lanka (d) Bhutan

53 Clara Furse is the first woman to become a CEO in the 228 year history of:
(a) NASDAQ (b) BSE
(c) NSE (d) New York Stock Exchange

54 On February 8, 2001, Insurgents of Dima Halong Danga group killed nine policemen in a remote place in:
(a) Madhya Pradesh (b) Assam
(c) Tamil Nadu (d) Arunachal Pradesh

55 The normal States get their assistance in the ratio of 70 per cent loan and 30 per cent grant whereas Special Category State status would provide Central assistance in the form of 90 per cent grant and 10 per cent loan. The Special Category Status has been given to:
(a) Uttaranchal (b) Jharkhand
(c) Chattisgarh (d) Bihar

56 The provision for subsidy made in 2001-02 is Rs. .... crore against 12000 crore of 2000-01
(a) 12675 (b) 13675

(c) 13657 (d) 13576

57 Which is the following aluminium company leads in production (in the year 2000)

(a) NALCO (b) HINDALCO
(c) BALCO (d) MALCO

58 'Aasman Aur Bhi Hain' is a book written by:'

(a) Tasleema Nasreen (b) Mridula Kalan
(c) Arundhati Roy (d) None of these

59 The newly appointed U.S. ambassador to India is:

(a) Robert D. Blackwill (b) Richard Celeste
(c) George W. Bush (d) None of these

60 The World Cup Football 2010 will be held in:

(a) Russia (b) Argentina
(c) France (d) South Africa

61 According to Census 2001, as on March 1, 2001, the population of India stood at:

(a) 1027,010,247 (b) 1027,015,247
(c) 1028,015,247 (d) None of these

62 What is the capital of Chattisgarh?

(a) Panaji (b) Ranchi
(c) Raipur (d) None of these

63 Who is the Governor of Delhi?

(a) Mrs. Meera Kumar
(b) Mrs. Sheila Dikshit
(c) Mr. Vijay Kumar Kapoor
(d) Mrs. Shanti Desai

64 Which of the following is not an objective of India's economy?

(a) Population Growth (b) Industrial Growth
(c) Self Reliance (d) Employment Generation

65 Who is the Chairman of the newly Constituted Task Force on Information Technology?

(a) Pramod Mahajan (b) Arun Jaitley
(c) Ram Vilas Paswan (d) Murli Manohar Joshi

66 National Games 2001 will be held in Punjab from:

(a) September 16 - 29 (b) August 16 - 29
(c) June 16 - 29 (d) July 16 - 29

67 India won four Gold Medals in the Asian Powerlifting Championship which was held in:
(a) Mumbai (b) Punjab
(c) Bangalore (d) Delhi

68 With which Company batting maestro Sachin Tendulkar signs a five year contract for Rs. 80 crore?
(a) Pepsi (b) World Tel
(c) Adidas (d) None of these

69 Which Indain Cricketer holds the unique record of three consequitive centuries in the first three tests?
(a) Saurav Ganguly (b) Mohammad Azharuddin
(c) Surinder Amarnath (d) Gundappa Vishwanath

70 In which field Chameli Award is awarded?
(a) Journalism (b) Sports
(c) Music (d) Book

71 Name the website which broke the cricket match fixing story earlier this year:
(a) bazee.com (b) tehelka.com
(c) goforcricket.com (d) None of these

72 Who wrote the book 'The Cinemas of India' ?
(a) Arundhati Roy (b) Yves Thoraval
(c) Ms. Hillary Clinton (d) None of these

73 Who wrote the book 'An Invention to the White House' ?
(a) Ms. Hillary Clinton (b) Yves Thoraval
(c) Bill Clinton (d) None of these

74 Which country is to host The First Afro Asian Games in 2001
(a) India (b) Japan
(c) South Africa (d) Egypt

75 Name the player who has been banned from playing Cricket for five years:
(a) Nikhil Chopra (b) Ajay Jadeja
(c) Ajay Sharma (d) Mohammad Azharuddin

76 Devyani, for whose sake Dipendra shot and killed all his family members belongs to:
(a) India (b) Nepal
(c) Pakistan (d) England

77 Where were the first Asian Games held?
(a) Seoul (b) New Delhi
(c) Beijing (d) Colombo

78 Legendary Cricketer, Sir Donald Bradman who passed away at the age of 92 on:
(a) November 26, 2000 (b) December 26, 2000
(c) January 26, 2000 (d) February 26, 2000

79 Who is the first Indian player in 21 years to win the All England Badminton Open title?
(a) Prakash Padukone (b) Leander Paes
(c) Pullela Gopichand (d) None of these

80 Who is the Foreign Sercretary of India?
(a) Jaswant Singh (b) Chokila Iyer
(c) Mr. Krishna Kant (d) None of these

81 Who is the Chairman of Planning Commission?
(a) K. C. Pant (b) C. Rangarajan
(c) Atal Behari Vajpayee (d) None of these

82 'Rano-O-Bhanu' the book dwells on Tagore's relationship with Lady Ranu Mukherjee who died in the year 2000 is written by:
(a) Sunil Gangopadhyaye (b) Bankim Chandra Chatterjee
(c) Aurobindo Ghosh (d) None of these

83 Gandhi's Legacy 'The Life and Legacy of Mahatma Gandhi' is written by:
(a) Khushwant Singh (b) Nelson Mandela
(c) Stanley Wolpert (d) None of these

84 Late Mr. Dewang Mehta who recently died of a heart attack in a hotel in Sydney was the President of:
(a) Infosys (b) IBM
(c) NASSCOM (d) None of these

85 Who is the Chairman of the UN Human Rights Committee?
(a) Justice P. N. Bhagwati (b) Mr. Y. K. Chaturvedi
(c) S. C. Gupta (d) None of these

86 Sir Donald Bradman, the legendary cricketer who passed away belongs to which country?
(a) Australia (b) South Africa
(c) England (d) West Indies

87 Who has been voted 'The man of the year 2000' ?
(a) Amitabh Bachchan (b) Shahrukh Khan
(c) Sachin Tendulkar (d) Atal Behari Vajpaye

88 Pullela Gopichand became the first Indian player in 21 years to win the All England Badminton Open title after defeating:
(a) Chen Hong (b) Michel Chang
(c) Thangre Jaidee (d) None of these

89 The 73rd Oscar Award for Best Director was given to:
(a) Steven Speilberg (b) Steven Soderberg
(c) John Fleming (d) None of these

90 The 73rd Oscar Award for Best Actor was given to:
(a) Arnold Shwarzenneger (b) Keanu Reeves
(c) Russell Crowe (d) Leonardo Di Caprio

91 The 73rd Oscar Award for Best Actress was given to:
(a) Kate Winslet (b) Julia Roberts
(c) Julia Walters (d) None of these

92 The 48th National Film Awards were announced by the Chairperson of the Jury:
(a) Amitabh Bachchan (b) Ms. Vyajanthimala Bali
(c) Dilip Kumar (d) Dev Anand

93 The 48th National Film Awards were announced on:
(a) April 27, 2001 (b) February 27, 2001
(c) March 27, 2001 (d) May 27, 2001

94 The 48th National Film Awards were held in:
(a) Mumbai (b) Bangalore
(c) Kolkata (d) New Delhi

95 The 48th National Best Film Award was given to the film:
(a) Shantam (b) Daman
(c) Pukar (d) Utsab

96 The 48th National Best Director Award was given to:
(a) Rituparna (b) J. P. Dutta
(c) Kalpana Lajmi (d) Jayaraj

97 The 48th National Best Music Director Award was given to:
(a) Nadeem - Shrawan (b) Anu Malik
(c) Lalit Sen - Samir Sen (d) Rajesh Roshan

98 The 48th National Best Male Playback Singer Award was given to:
(a) Udit Narayan (b) Sonu Nigam
(c) Shanker Mahadevan (d) Kumar Sanu

99 The 48th National Best Female Playback Singer Award was given to:
(a) Alka Yagnik (b) Asha Bhonsle
(c) Bhavatharini R. (d) Lata Mangeshkar

100 The 48th National Integration Award was given to:
(a) Daman (b) Pukar
(c) Border (d) Zubeida

101 The 48th National Best Film Award was given to:
(a) Refugee (b) Pukar
(c) Zubeida (d) Daman

102 The 48th National Best Actress Award was given to:
(a) Karishma Kapoor (b) Raveena Tondon
(c) Tabu (d) Nandita Das

103 The 48th National Best Actor Award was given to:
(a) Anil Kapoor (b) Shahrukh Khan
(c) Hritik Roshan (d) Aamir Khan

104 Anil Kapoor was awarded the best actor award for the film:
(a) Pukar (b) Taal
(c) Biwi No. 1 (d) Mann

105 Raveena Tandon was awarded the best actress award for the film:
(a) Shool (b) Ghulam-E-Mustafa
(c) Daman (d) Dilwale

106 The Oscar awards were announced on:
(a) March 26, 2001 (b) January 26, 2001
(c) February 26, 2001 (d) May 26, 2001

107 The Oscar awards were announced in the year 2001 were:
(a) 71st Annual Academy Awards
(b) 75th Annual Academy Awards
(c) 70th Annual Academy Awards
(d) 73rd Annual Academy Awards

108 The 73rd Oscar Award for Best Picture was given to:
(a) Gladiator (b) The Hollow Man
(c) The 6th Day (d) American Beauty

109 Who won the Embassy World Snooker Championship in England?
(a) Ronnie O' Sullivan (b) John Haggins
(c) Lee Bong Ju (d) Silvio Guerra

110 Who won the World Proffesional Billiards Championship in May 2001?
(a) Mike Russel (b) Peter Gilchrist
(c) Heath Streak (d) Bear Grylls

111 Name the country who won the Asia Cup 2001 Badminton Championship?
(a) China (b) Korea
(c) England (d) Thailand

112 Name the country who won the Sharjah Triangular One Day Series?
(a) India (b) Pakistan
(c) Sri Lanka (d) New Zealand

113 Who won the Ranji Trophy of 2001?
(a) Mumbai (b) Baroda
(c) Hyderabad (d) Gujarat

114 Name the highest Wicket taker in Test Cricket who announced his retirement from the Test Cricket:
(a) Kapil Dev (b) Wasim Akram
(c) Allan Donald (d) Courtney Walsh

115 Which country created a new world record in Football history defeating Samoa with 31 - 0 goals in the Oceania World Cup Football Qualifier held at Coffs Harbour, Australia ?
(a) Korea (b) Australia
(c) West Indies (d) England

116 Who was the runner up of Mackyung LG Fashion Open Golf Tournament at South Korea on April 29, 2001 ?
(a) India (b) Pakistan
(c) China (d) Sri Lanka

117 Who won the 46 World Table Tennis Championship?
(a) Japan (b) China
(c) Korea (d) Spain

118 Who Clinch the US Clay Court Championship of 2001 ?
(a) India (b) Korea
(c) Spain (d) China

119 Name the cricketer who was honoured with Maharashtra Bhushan on April 24, 2001:
(a) Saurav Ganguly (b) Anil Kumble
(c) Sachin Tendulkar (d) Gilchrist

120 Who was crowned Miss Universe for 2001?
(a) Miss India (Celina Jaitley)
(b) Miss Greece (Evelina Papanto Kruenger)
(c) Miss Puerto Rico (Denise Ominozes)
(d) Thailand

121 Which month SLV was launched?
(a) March 2001 (b) April 2001
(c) January 2001 (d) May 2001

122 On 5th May 2001 India has launched a new Military operation, what is the name of the miliary operation?
(a) Vijay (b) Operation Vijay
(c) Poorna Vijay (d) Victory

123 Who has been appointed as part time Chairman of the Rail Tel. Corporation, a project to cover the entire 65,000 Km of railway network in the country?
(a) Mr. P. Chidambaram (b) Mr. N. K. Chidambaram

124 SLV was Re-launched successfully on:
(a) April 18 (b) May 18
(c) March 18 (d) February 18

125 Who is the person who became the first Space Tourist in the World?
(a) Dennis Tito (b) Yuri Butarin
(c) Talgat Musabayer (d) Martin Mong

126 Who is the Cricketer to set the record of highest individual score 281 in Test Cricket?
(a) V. V. S. Laxman (b) Sachin Tendulkar
(c) Saurav Ganguly (d) Rahul Dravid

127 Name the website which broke the cricket matchfixing story this year:
(a) bazee.com (b) goforcricket.com
(c) tehelka.com (d) tazakhabar.com

128 Who is credited with the idea of linking each page of information on the net to another that went on to create the world wide web (www)

(a) Al Gore (b) Bill Gates
(c) Tim Berners Lee (d) Steve Jobs

129 Who has recently been appointed the Chief of the Scheduled Tribes and Scheduled Castes penel
(a) Mangat Ram (b) Karia Munda
(c) Vijay Singh Bhuria (d) Vijay Oraon

130 The first electric car in India has been launched recently by a Bangalore based company. The name of the car is
(a) RAVEN (b) RITA
(c) REVA (d) REVATHI

131 According to the Lussane based IMD ranking the position of India is
(a) 25th (b) 41st
(c) 46th (d) 72nd

132 The Saraswati Samman was presented to Dr. Indira Parthasarathy for her play
(a) Agastya (b) Shankaracharya
(c) Maduraikanda (d) Ramanujar

133 Belgaon was in the news because of a boarder dispute which the Concerned states of
(a) Maharashtra and Karnataka
(b) Gujarat and Maharashtra
(c) Karnataka and Tamil Nadu
(d) Karnataka and Andhra Pradesh

134 A Pureto Ricon has become the Miss Universe 2001, she is
(a) Kandace Krueger (b) Eva Quinones
(c) Denise Quinones (d) Evelina Papantoniou

135 The joint army and airforce exercise held in the desert at Rajasthan was code named
(a) Poorna Vijay (b) Vijayadoot
(c) Poorna Kranti (d) Sampurna Vijay

136 Assembly elections were held on May 10, 2001 in Tamil Nadu, Assam, West Bengal, Kerla and
(a) Maharashtra (b) Pondicherry
(c) Daman and Diu (d) Bihar

137 The next Chief election commissioner to replace Mr. M. S. Gill

on June 13, is

(a0 Mr. S. Shastri (b) Mr. P. Hazarika

(c) Mr. J. M. Lyngdoh (d) Mr. B. B. Tandon

138 The book 'India's China Pe.:spective' has been written by

(a) K. Natwar Singh (b) Chandra Shekhar

(c) K. R. Narayanan (d) Subhramanium Swamy

139 The centre has recently fixed pa particular day to be celeberated every year as anti-terrarrism day. The day is

(a) May 16 (b) May 18

(c) May 21 (d) May 25

140 The commission which is in the news because of the Israel-Pelestinian violence is

(a) Mitchell Commission

(b) Perez Commission

(c) Ralph Commission

(d) Rudalf Commission

141 The tallest building in the world at present is in Kualalumpur. It is known as

(a) Skyline towers (b) King towers

(c) Abu Benem towers (d) Petronas tower

142 The Golden Palm Award at the 54th Cannes Film Festival has been bagged by

(a) The son's room

(b) No man's land

(c) Mulholland drive

(d) The man who was not there

143 Which militant outfit was banned by the centre on May 3, 2001, for its activities in Andhra Pradesh, Karnataka and Goa?

(a) SIMI (b) Deenar Anjuman

(c) Joish Mohammad (d) Harkat-ul-Ansar

144 49 least developed countries had a conference on May 13, 2001 at which of the following places?

(a) Dhaka (b) Geneva

(c) Brussels (d) Kathmandu

145 The prize money for the nobel prize 2001, has been increased by \$100,000. It is now stands at (in swidish crowns)

(a) 10 million (b) 11 million

(c) 12 million (d) 13 million

146 A controversial plan for unification of Europe has been put forward recently. The propounder of the plan is
(a) Jacqueous Chirac (b) Gerhard Shroeder
(c) Bon hardt Williams (d) Tony Blair

147 The mascot for the FIFA Worldcup kto be held in 2002 Seoul is
(a) Pik, Nik, Tao (b) Chun, Mun, Tao
(c) Wen, Wei, Wow (d) Nik, Kaz, Ato

148 The per capita outstanding debt of India as on March 2000, stood at
(a) Rs. 4,672 (b) Rs. 10,254
(c) Rs. 10,549 (d) Rs. 11,539

149 On April 29, therewas a massive fire outbreak in an ammunition dump
(a) Kanpur (b) Kapurthala
(c) Pathankot (d) Jabalpur

150 The G-24 meet of the finance ministers of twenty four developing countries was held at
(a) New Delhi (b) Dhaka
(c) Madrid (d) Washington

151 Which country has recently been voted out at the UN Human Rights Commission and drugs panel board?
(a) Iraq (b) China
(c) Vietnam (d) US

152 Which among the following states has recently been conferred the status of special category state?
(a) Jharkhand (b) Chhtisgarh
(c) Uttaranchal (d) Sikkim

153 The Russian built Osa missile was test fired successfully on May 3, from interim test range at Chandipur, Orissa, is a
(a) Air to air missile
(b) Air to surface missile
(c) S urface to air missile
(d) Surface to surface missile

154 The first Crorepati couple at the famous series Kaun Banega Crorepati are

(a) Mrs. Arundhati and Mr. Vijay Paul
(b) Mrs. Mohindi and Mr. Aditya Chopra
(c) Mrs. Vaidehi and Mr. Chand kapoor
(d) Mrs. Shruti and Mr. Pankaj Jain

155 EmmoliSharifovic, who visited India on May 10, is the President of which country?
(a) Kysghistan (b) Uzbekistan
(c) Tajikistan (d) Armenia

156 The recently launched product NEVA is a
(a) Contraceptive pill (b) HIV detection kit
(c) Hybrid rice (d) Small Computer

157 On May 12, 2001, the Reserve Bank of India reduced the cash reserve ration by o.5 percentage points to
(a) 6.5 (b) 7.0
(c) 7.5 (d) 8.0

158 According to national Sample Survey organisation the percentage of people living below poverty line is
(a) 26.1% (b) 27.3%
(c) 32.4% (d) 33.9%

159 The approach paper of the tenth plan (2002-07) has proposed that the plan should aim at the GDP growth rate of
(a) 7% (b) 8%
(c) 8.2% (d) 8.7%

160 A veteran of the Indian National Army (INA) passed away on May 18, 2001. He was
(a) Mohan Singh (b) Ratan Singh
(c) Shishir Bose (d) Pratyush Ghosh

161 A leading wicket-keeper of India announced his retirement from International Cricket. He is
(a) Nayan Mongia (b) Sameer Dighe
(c) R. Prasad (d) Saba Karim

162 A sanskrit tradition theatre has been declared as masterpiece of the oral and intangible heritage of humanity by UNESCO. This theatre is
(a) Padripattu (b) Koodiyattam
(c) Veluattam (d) Ponnuraikutty

163 The newly appointed director of the Intelligence Bureau is
(a) Mr. D. P. Singh (b) Mr. V. S. Rao
(c) Mr. K. P. Singh (d) Mr. P. N. Tripathi

164 Who is the new king of Nepal after the assacination of previous king?
(a) Dipendra Bir Bibram Shah Dev
(b) Gyaendra Bir Bikram S hah Dev
(c) Mahendra Bir Bikram Shah Dev
(d) None of these

165 Prince of Nepal Dipendra gunned down his family members on
(a) June 3, 2001 (b) June 2, 2001
(c) June 1, 2001 (d) None of these

166 Late king Birendra Bikram Shah Dev was monarch since
(a) 1975 (b) 1974
(c) 1973 (d) 1972

167 Who is the newly elected Chief Minister of Tamil nadu
(a) Karunanidhi (b) Karunakaran
(c) Jayalalitha (d) None of these

168 Who is the director of film Lagaan
(a) Amir Khan (b) Ashutosh Gowariker
(c) Anil Sharma (d) None of these

169 Who is the winner of All England Badminton Championship 2001?
(a) Prakash Podukone (b) Leander Paes
(c) Gopichand (d) None of these

170 The author of the book "Land Relation and Agrarian Development in India" is
(a) Niranjan Mishra (b) Shakti Prasad Padhi
(c) Asit Sen (d) None of these

171 Microsoft Windows Millennium Edition to be launched shortly nicknamed as—
(a) Micr (b) Win
(c) Windows Me (d) Soft

172 Which of the following states has highest number of child labour
(a) Andhra Pradesh (b) Uttar Pradesh
(c) West Bengal (d) Madhya Pradesh

173 In how many states Assembly election were held in May 2001

(a) 1 (b) 5
(c) 6 (d) None of these

174 Who is the newly appointed coach of Indian Cricket Team?
(a) Greg Chappel (b) Jeof Marsh
(c) John Wright (d) Dean Jones

175 Who is the new President of Maxico?
(a) Mr. Ernesto Zedillo (b) Mr. Vicent Fox
(c) Johonnes rau (d) None of these

176 Who among the following is the present Chairman of ISRO
(a) R. Chidambaram
(b) A. P. J. Abdul Kalam
(c) Prof. K. Kasturirangam
(d) Prof. Satish Dhawan

177 Who among the folowing is the present President of USA?
(a) George Bush (b) George W. Bush
(c) Bill Clinton (d) Ronald Reagan

178 Who is the present President of South Africa?
(a) Thabo Mbeki (b) Jacob Juna
(c) Nelson Mandela (d) Kofi Annan

179 Which of the following two countries are the largest Uranium producers in the world:
(a) Italy and Spain
(b) Peru and Russia
(c) USA and Russia
(d) USA and canada

180 Foreign aid will:
(a) Raise the level of investment
(b) Be used to enlarge technical resources
(c) Be used for building up industries
(d) All of the above

181 Who wrote the General Theory of Employment, Interst and Money?
(a) Kaldor (b) Marx
(c) Keynes (d) Marshall

182 Recently Macau, a Portuguese colony was reverted to:
(a) China (b) Indonesia
(c) Japan (d) Thailand

183 Harry Potler who was recently in news is a famous:
(a) Cine Actor (b) Film Director
(c) Author (d) Pop singer

184 Why was R. R. Gopal in the news recently:
(a) He has been nominated for Rajya sabha
(b) Hae has been inducted as Minister of State in the capital
(c) He acted as a mediator between Veerappan and the Government
(d) None of these

185 Prof. Amartya Sen was in the news because:
(a) He is internationally known as a social economist
(b) He has been awarded 'Bharat Ratna'
(c) He is a recipient of the Nobel Prize
(d) All of above

186 Which of the following countries recently launched a new range of ballistic missile called the 'Ghauri'
(a) China (b) Pakistan
(c) Russia (d) India

187 Taj group of hotel is owned by
(a) Birlas (b) Goenkas
(c) Hindujas (d) Tatas

188 Who among the following has been appointed as the Brand Ambassador of Omega brand of watches belonging to Swiss Watch Group:
(a) Salman Khan (b) Mel Gibson
(c) Jacky Chan (d) Shah Rukh Khan

189 World's oldest operating oil refinery is located in:
(a) Gujarat (b) U. P.
(c) Assam (d) None of the above

190 Who is the present United nation's security general:
(a) Boutras Boutras Ghali
(b) Kofi Annan
(c) Nelson Mendala
(d) None of these

191 According to C.B.I charge-sheet, Hinduja Brothers had received 81 million Swedish Kroners (10 million dollors) from Bofors which bagged the Rs. 1437 crore Bofors gun contract in:

(a) 1980 (b) 1982
(c) 1984 (d) 1986

192 Bharat Ratna, India's highest civillian award 2001 was conferred on:
(a) Ravi Shankar and Amartya Sen
(b) M. S. Subulakshmi and C. Subramanium
(c) Lata Mangeshkar and Ustad Bismillah Khan
(d) Satyajit ray and Dr. A. P. J. Abdul Kalam

193 Enron Development Corporation which has been allowed bigger stake in Dabhol corporation's power project is:
(a) UK.-based (b) US-based
(c) Russia-based (d) Germany-based

194 Dbhol Power Project is in:
(a) Tamil Nadu (b) Maharashtra
(c) Madhya Pradesh (d) Andhra Pradesh

195 On January 4, 2001, India is successfully launched maiden test flight of the indigeneous Light Combat Aircraft from:
(a) Bangalore (b) Mumbai
(c) New Delhi (d) Hyderabad

196 International Day for persons with disabilities is observed on:
(a) January 1 (b) March 30
(c) December 3 (d) October 4

197 National Consumer Day is observed on:
(a) September 4 (b) October 5
(c) November 11 (d) December 24

198 Name the person who has been appointed Ambassador of ICICI for two years:
(a) Shahrukh Khan (b) Amitabh Bachchan
(c) Salman Khan (d) None of these

199 In which state the National Gallery of Modern Art — (NGMA) located?
(a) Delhi (b) Mumbai
(c) Kolkata (d) Bangalore

200 What is HIV Positive:
(a) A modern music instrument
(b) The name of a USA's Passanger's flight

(c) An electricity rays
(d) A cause of AIDS disease

201 The target for US investment in India in the next year (2001-02) has been fixed at:
(a) $ 2 billion (b) $ 1 billion
(c) $ 5 billion (d) $ 10 billion

202 'Value and Capital' is written by:
(a) V. P. Minnhas (b) Kins
(c) Adam Smith (d) Hicks

203 In which city, the World Cup Football 2002 is decided to play:
(a) Tokyo (b) Nagasaki
(c) Yakohama (d) Hiroshima

204 What is the nick name of Rahul Dravid:
(a) Jet (b) Jambo
(c) Jemmy (d) Babu

205 Low service, high service, lift, service break and love, belongs to which sport:
(a) Tennis (b) Badminton
(c) Cricket (d) Basketball

206 Name the writer of 'Waiting for Mahatma':
(a) R. K. Narayan (b) Khushwant Singh
(c) Mukulraj Anand (d) Neerad C. Chaudhary

207 Who is the Indian Cricketer to have scored 3 centuries in a row in his first test matches:
(a) Sachin Tendulkar (b) Kapil Dev
(c) Mohd. Azharuddin (d) Sunil Gavaskar

208 The cricketer who acts in a T.V. Serial, is:
(a) Salil Ankola (b) Nilesh Kulkarni
(c) Abbey Kuruvilla (d) Nobody

209 What is the nick name of Anil Kumble
(a) Jimmy (b) Jammy
(c) Jumbo (d) Jet

210 'Malti Madhav' is written by:
(a) Wakpati (b) Bhavbooti
(c) Parimal Gupt (d) Hari Suri

211 First One Day International Cricket was played at:
(a) Sydney (b) Lords
(c) Melbourn (d) Capetown

212 'Chaina Mann' word is related to:
(a) Polo (b) Cricket
(c) Badminton (d) Hockey

213 Who is the main male character of famous novel 'Godan'
(a) Hori (b) Mirza Khursheed
(c) Rai Saheb (d) Gover

214 Name the state in India which was hit by Earthquake on Jan, 26, 2001:
(a) Gujarat (b) Assam
(c) Maharashtra (d) Arunanchal Pradesh

215 Name the country whose Prince Dependra Bir Bikram Shah Dev has killed all his family members:
(a) Nepal (b) Bhutan
(c) England (d) China

216 Which player is known as'Bombay Bomber':
(a) Saurav Ganguli (b) Sachin Tendulkar
(c) Rahul Dravid (d) None of these

217 In which city famous football stadium 'Chandrshekharam Nayar' is situated?
(a) Trivendrum (b) Bangalore
(c) Chennai (d) Mumbai

218 American Cup is related to:
(a) Vacrering (b) Golf
(c) Chess (d) Badminton

219 Indira: The life of Indira Nehru. Who wrote this book?
(a) Katherine Frank (b) Arundhati Roy
(c) R. K. Narayan (d) Abdul Kalam Azad

220 Who wrote the book named 'Stability in South Asia'?
(a) T. S. Eliot (b) Frenz Kalka
(c) Vishnu Sharma (d) Ashley J. Tellis

221 Name the writer of 'Facing Up'
(a) Kantherine (b) Bear Grylls
(c) Kuldip Nayar (d) Serena Williams

222 Name the director, who is working on a film on the life and times of Nelson Mandela?
(a) John Wu (b) Martin Scorcese
(c) Steven Speilberg (d) Shekhar Kapoor

223 Name the author who wrote the book called 'People like us'?
(a) Pawan Kumar Verma
(b) Shankar Dayal Sharma
(c) Atal Bihari Vajpayee
(d) K. R. Narayanan

224 'A Gift of Wings' is written by:
(a) Shanti Gopalan (b) Shanti Kumar
(c) Arundhati Roy (d) None of these

225 Which of the country has hosted the first Afro-Asian Games in 2001:
(a) India (b) Japan
(c) South Africa (d) Egypt

226 Who is the author of the famous book 'Midnight's Children'?
(a) Salman Rushdie (b) Vikram Seth
(c) V. S. Naipal (d) Nayantara Sehgal

227 What is the position of the cricket field right behind the wicket-keeper on the boundary?
(a) Long spot (b) Long cover
(c) Short spot (d) None of these

228 In which city Eden Garden Stadium is located?
(a) Mumbai (b) Kolkata
(c) New Delhi (d) Bangalore

229 How many players are in every 'Handball' team?
(a) 10 (b) 12
(c) 8 (d) 11

230 Who is the new President of America?
(a) George Bush (b) George W. Bush
(c) Bill Clinton (d) Charles Wald

231 Quelzal is the currency of
(a) French Guyana (b) West Indies
(c) Guatemala (d) Luxemburg

232 The name of Pandit Ravi Shankar is associated with:

(a) Sarod (b) Sitar
(c) Veena (d) Violin

233 Who is the author of the book "Preparing for the twenty first century"?
(a) Henery Kissinger (b) V. R. Kennedy
(c) V. R. Krishan Iyer (d) V. S. Naipal

234 Wimbeldon is a place connected with
(a) Cricket (b) Lawn Tennis
(c) Badminton (d) Table Tennis

235 'Durgesh Nandit' was written by:
(a) Sarat Chandra (b) Bankim Chandra
(c) Tara Shankar (d) Tagore

236 'A Suitable Boy' was written by:
(a) R. K. Narayan (b) Mulk Raj Anand
(c) Arundhati Roy (d) Vikram Seth

237 Who is the author of 'The Judgement'?
(a) R. Venkatraman (b) Kuldip Rhakur
(c) Anthony Masarenas (d) Janardan Thakur

238 What is the name of the new European Currency?
(a) Euro Dollor (b) Pound
(c) Sterling (d) Euro

239 Dollor is the currency of all the following countries except:
(a) Jamaica (b) New Zealand
(c) Guyana (d) None of these

240 Currency of South Africa is:
(a) Rand (b) Shekel
(c) Pound (d) Guilder

241 The currency of Indonesia is :
(a) Rial (b) Bhat
(c) Dinar (d) Rupiah

242 Ustad Bismillah Khan is related to:
(a) Sitar (b) Guitar
(c) Shehnai (d) Hindustani (Classical)

243 Name the author of 'Worshiping False Gods'?
(a) Khushwant Singh (b) Arundhati Roy

(c) Salman Rushdie (d) Arun Shourie

244 Name the currency of Russia:
(a) Dollor (b) Pound
(c) Euro (d) Rubal

245 What is the name of winner (Miss India-Universe) in 2001:
(a) Celina Jetley (b) Sara Corner
(c) Lara Dutta (d) Maheshwari

246 In which city Nagarhole National Park is situated?
(a) Bangalore (b) Chandigarh
(c) Goa (d) Mysore

247 Term 'Hattrick' is related to:
(a) Hockey (b) Table Tennis
(c) Football (d) Cricket

248 Name the author of 'Communist Maniferto':
(a) Karl Marx and Fredric Engels.
(b) Khushwant Singh
(c) Shakespeare
(d) Arundhati Roy

249 Which is known to be the oldest sport:
(a) Cricket (b) Kabbaddi
(c) Hockey (d) Archery

250 Which is the National Sport of Spain?
(a) Football (b) Hockey
(c) Tennis (d) Bull-fighting

251 Mahakumbh 2001was held at:
(a) Agra (b) Hyderabad
(c) Allahabad (d) Haridwar

252 The currency of Thailand is:
(a) Dinar (b) Rial
(c) Yen (d) Bhat

253 Name of the author of Ramaya Darshan:
(a) G. Shankar Kurup
(b) V. Satyanarayan
(c) K. V. Puttapa
(d) T. S. Pillai

254 Name the auther who wrote 'The Hindu View of Life':
(a) S. Radhakrishnan
(b) Sri Aurobindo
(c) Rabindra Nath Tagore
(d) Swami Vivekanand

255 Name the country which will host next Commonwealth Games:
(a) Mauritius (b) Malayasia
(c) Sri Lanka (d) India

256 'Discovery of India' was written by:
(a) Jawahrlal Nehru
(b) Sardar Vallabhbhai Patel
(c) M. K. Gandhi
(d) C. Rajgopalachari

257 'The God of Small Things' is written by:
(a) Arundhati Ghosh (b) Arundhati Roy
(c) Salman Rushdie (d) Pashupati

258 Common currency of Europeon Community is:
(a) Euro (b) Dollor
(c) Dinar (d) Cent

259 Merdeka cup is related to:
(a) Cricket (b) Football
(c) Chess (d) Hockey

260 India's first Nobel Prize winner is:
(a) Rabindra Nath Tagore
(b) Mahatma Gandhi
(c) Bankim Chandra Chatterjee
(d) Moti Lal Nehru

Answers

1	(b)	2	(d)	3	(c)	4	(d)	5	(4)
6	(c)	7	(d)	8	(c)	9	(c)	10	(b)
11	(b)	12	(b)	13	(b)	14	(c)	15	(d)
16	(d)	17	(c)	18	(a)	19	(d)	20	(4)
21	(a)	22	(c)	23	(c)	24	(d)	25	(d)
26	(b)	27	(a)	28	(a)	29	(c)	30	(b)
31	(c)	32	(c)	33	(c)	34	(a)	35	(d)
36	(a)	37	(c)	38	(c)	39	(a)	40	(b)
41	(a)	42	(a)	43	(c)	44	(c)	45	(b)
46	(b)	47	(b)	48	(c)	49	(b)	50	(d)
51	(a)	52	(b)	53	(d)	54	(b)	55	(a)
56	(b)	57	(c)	58	(b)	59	(a)	60	(d)
61	(b)	62	(c)	63	(c)	64	(c)	65	(a)
66	(a)	67	(d)	68	(b)	69	(b)	70	(a)
71	(b)	72	(b)	73	(a)	74	(a)	75	(b)
76	(a)	77	(b)	78	(d)	79	(c)	80	(b)
81	(c)	82	(a)	83	(c)	84	(c)	85	(a)
86	(a)	87	(d)	88	(a)	89	(b)	90	(c)
91	(b)	92	(b)	93	(c)	94	(d)	95	(a)
96	(a)	97	(b)	98	(c)	99	(c)	100	(b)
101	(c)	102	(b)	103	(a)	104	(a)	105	(c)
106	(a)	107	(d)	108	(a)	109	(a)	110	(b)
111	(a)	112	(c)	113	(b)	114	(d)	115	(b)
116	(a)	117	(b)	118	(a)	119	(c)	120	(d)
121	(a)	122	(c)	123	(d)	124	(a)	125	(a)
126	(a)	127	(c)	128	(b)	129	(b)	130	(c)
131	(b)	132	(d)	133	(a)	134	(c)	135	(a)
136	(b)	137	(d)	138	(d)	139	(c)	140	(a)

141	(d)	142	(a)	143	(b)	144	(c)	145	(a)
146	(b)	147	(d)	148	(d)	149	(c)	150	(d)
151	(d)	152	(a)	153	(c)	154	(a)	155	(c)
156	(b)	157	(c)	158	(a)	159	(b)	160	(b)
161	(d)	162	(b)	163	(c)	164	(b)	165	(c)
166	(d)	167	(c)	168	(b)	169	(c)	170	(a)
171	(c)	172	(a)	173	(b)	174	(c)	175	(b)
176	(c)	177	(b)	178	(a)	179	(d)	180	(d)
181	(c)	182	(a)	183	(c)	184	(c)	185	(d)
186	(b)	187	(d)	188	(d)	189	(c)	190	(b)
191	(d)	192	(c)	193	(b)	194	(b)	195	(a)
196	(c)	197	(d)	198	(b)	199	(a)	200	(d)
201	(a)	202	(d)	203	(c)	204	(c)	205	(b)
205	(a)	207	(c)	208	(a)	209	(c)	210	(b)
211	(c)	212	(b)	213	(a)	214	(a)	215	(a)
216	(b)	217	(a)	218	(a)	219	(a)	220	(d)
221	(b)	222	(d)	223	(a)	224	(a)	225	(a)
226	(a)	227	(b)	228	(b)	229	(b)	230	(b)
231	(c)	232	(b)	233	(b)	234	(b)	235	(b)
236	(d)	237	(b)	238	(d)	239	(d)	240	(a)
241	(d)	242	(c)	243	(a)	244	(d)	245	(a)
246	(d)	247	(d)	248	(a)	249	(d)	250	(d)
251	(c)	252	(d)	253	(a)	254	(a)	255	(b)
256	(a)	257	(b)	258	(a)	259	(b)	260	(a)

GENERAL AWARENESS

1 Who is the richest person in the world?
(a) Bill Gates
(b) Robson Walton
(c) Gopichand Hinduja

2 What is a generic drug?
(a) A medicine not covered by a patent.
(b) A drug normally becomes a generic drug when the patent on the drug lapses.
(c) The word generic is the scientific name of the drug.

3 ZVTS is a radial tyre being manufactured by which company?
(a) MRF
(b) JK
(c) Ceat

4 Mr. Arjun Malhotra, Chairman and CEO and co-founder of the HCL group has recently been honoured with :
(a) Padmashree
(b) Maharashtra Bhushan Award
(c) Albert Einstein Techrology Medal

5 Who is the manufacturer of Laughing Cow cheese?
(a) Amul
(b) Cadburys
(c) Fromageries Bel

6 What do you mean by email spam?
(a) Internet advertising
(b) Mass unsolicited emails
(c) Search engines

7 "From Thought to Finish" is a slogan of:
(a) Sterlite Industries
(b) MICO Bosch Group
(c) Ernst & Young

8 Bollywood sensation Hrithik Roshan is the brand ambassador for Tamarind. The name of the company which owns the brand?
(a) Reid & Taylor
(b) S. Kumars
(c) Raymonds

9 Name sportsman who became the first man ever to hold the four biggest tournament titles of his game at the same time and also top the list of America's wealthiest individuals.
(a) Michael Jordan
(b) Tiger Woods
(c) Pete Samprass

10 Trade name *Kraft* is associated with which of the following products?
(a) Cheese
(b) Tomato Ketchup
(c) Orange Juice

11 "Ab Ke Sawan" is the music album by :
(a) A. R. Rehman
(b) Subha Mudgal
(c) Euphoria

12 Name India's second largest pharma company that has offered a free supply of its AIDS drug for two years to the governmental organisations?
(a) Glaxo Smithkline
(b) Cipla
(c) Ranbaxy

13 Buena Vista Television India is a division of:
(a) Walt Disney India
(b) Zee Telefilms Ltd.
(c) New Delhi Televisions

14 What is the name of second music channel that MTV is considering to launch for the Indian sub-continent?
(a) MTV-Phir Se
(b) VH 1
(c) VTM

15 What is the name of the following film actresses is the brand ambassador for Lakme?
(a) Juhi Chawla
(b) Karishma Kapoor
(c) Lisa Ray

16 Parx is a leading garment brand of India. Who owns this brand?
(a) Raymonds

(b) Grasim
(c) Kothari

17 Who is the top boss of Sterlite Industries that has recently bought BALCO?
(a) Anil Agarwal
(b) Dhirubhai Ambani
(c) Rajan Kothari

18 Name the Managing Director of Enron India.
(a) Rebacca Marks
(b) Wade Cline
(c) Sanjay Bhatnagar

19 Limca Book of Records is owned by:
(a) Limca
(b) Boke
(c) Pepsi

20 Alitalia is the flag carrier of:
(a) Italy
(b) France
(c) Germany

21 What services are being provided by Spectranet?
(a) Cable TV network
(b) DTH network
(c) Broadband network

22 Name the largest selling motorcycle in India.
(a) TVS - Suzuki
(b) Hero Honda
(c) Bajaj

23 Name the author of the book IBM and the Holocaust.
(a) Bob woodward
(b) Edwin Black
(c) Amy Tan

24 Match the following:

(a) Veenu Srubuvasan	(i) CEO Royal Sun Alliance (RSA)
(b) Bob Mendelsohn	(ii) CEO TVS Suzuki
(c) Sunil Kapoor	(iii) Head of IT Fortis Health care

a. A1, B2, C3
b. A2, B1, C3
c A3, C2, B1

25 Plano digital flat TV is marketed by:
(a) Samsung
(b) Philips
(c) BPL

26 Who is the Executive Director of Jet Airways?
(a) Raj Bhatia
(b) Saroj Datta
(c) Pradeep Agal

27 As the private insurance juggernaut rolls on, which is the first company to hit the block?
(a) HDFC Standard Life
(b) Cholamandalam Distribution Services
(c) Indian Bank

28 Which of the following companies has been given licence for life insurance business?
(a) Reliance General
(b) Bajaj Allianze
(c) SBI Cardliff

29 Name the toothpaste which has now started using megastars to push volumes of its produce?
(a) Pepsodent
(b) Colgate
(c) Close-up

30 "Building telecom, building partnerships" is the punch line of:
(a) Bharti Enterprises Ltd.
(b) Spice Telecom
(c) Tata

31 Trikaya Grey, the advertising giant has recently changed its name to:
(a) Spectrum Communications
(b) Grey Worldwide
(c) Traditional Advertising Agency

32 Nihar coconut oil is a product of:

(a) Dabur
(b) Dabon International
(c) Hindustan Lever

33. Marketing Pundit's latest focus is on CRM. What does it stands for?
(a) Customer Relationship Management
(b) Competition Regulative Management
(c) Country Research Management

34 Small looks, big impact is the slogan from:
(a) HP Deskjet Printer
(b) Epson ultra portable projector
(c) Samsung

35 Azim Premji is the chairman of:
(a) Infosys
(b) Wipro
(c) Confederation of Indian Industry

36 Coca-Cola is moving its entire marketing operations from its corporate headquarters (Gurgaon, Haryana) to:
(a) New Delhi
(b) Mumbai
(c) Bangalore

37 Hindustan Motors is the manufacturers of which car?
(a) Mitsubishi Lancer
(b) Sonata
(c) Accord

38 Anand Rathi is:
(a) CII Chief
(b) Former BSE President
(c) Advocate General of Maharashtra

39 Which watch manufacturer has launched "Eco-Drive, the light-powered watch"?
(a) Citizen
(b) Swatch
(c) Titan

40 Havell's is the brand name associated with which type of products?
(a) Electrical products

(b) Auto parts
(c) Consumer products

41 "The Upper Crest" is the punch line of:
(a) Zodiac
(b) Raymond
(c) Louis Philippe

42 Hugo Boss is a trade name associated with:
(a) Perfume
(b) Cycles
(c) Travel Agency

43 Riz Khan, the famous TV anchor, represents which channel?
(a) Star TV
(b) BBC
(c) CNN

44 Vinod Mehta is the editor-in-chief of:
(a) A & M
(b) Cosmopolitan
(c) Outlook

45 Name the director-general of WTO:
(a) C. F. Patten
(b) Mike Moore
(c) Leo Burnett

46 The writing instruments major Parker has roped in which mega star as its latest brand endorser for multimedia campaign?
(a) Hrithik Roshan
(b) Amitabh Bachchan
(c) Shah Rukh Khan

47 Frost & Sullivan Market Engineering Award for Competitive Strategy 2001 in the Application Service Provider (ASP) Category has been won by:
(a) Wipro
(b) Satyam
(c) Rediff.com

48 "Live Smart" is the slogan of which newspaper?
(a) The Times of India
(b) Hindustan Times

(c) The Indian Express

49 Which bank was UTI Bank planning to acquire recently?
(a) HDFC
(b) Global Trust Bank
(c) Standard Chartered Bank

50 Name the Apple Computer CEO and co-founder
(a) Bill Gates
(b) Stephen Rakes
(c) Steve Job

51 Who among the following became the first administrator of the Union Territory of Chandigarh?
(a) Siddhartha Shankar Ray
(b) P. L. Thaper
(c) Darshan Singh Pheruman
(d) V. K. Menon

52 Which was the only Congress session presided by Mahatma Gandhi
(a) Surat
(b) Kolkata
(c) Lucknow
(d) Belgaum

53. Which Mugal emperor issued for the first time a square silver rupee known as the 'Jalali' named after him?
(a) Aurangzeb
(b) Akbar
(c) Jehangir
(d) Shahjehan

54 Which artist at Akbar's Court was known by the title 'Zerrin Kalam' or 'Golden Pen"?
(a) Mohammad Hussain
(b) Raja Birbal
(c) Abul Fazal
(d) Basawan

55 *Ben-Hur* was directed by
(a) William Hopkins
(b) William Wyler
(c) William Maclean
(d) Charles Schulz

56 Who among the following is the ICC President, who arrived in India during March 2001, to persuade the Indian Government to allow Pakistan play in India in the ICC Knock-out Cricket tournament?
(a) Malcom Grey
(b) Malcom Gaviria
(c) Carol Brown
(d) Louise Kochler

57 Bageshwari Qamar, the first and perhaps only woman Shahnai player in India, who has also got world wide recognition, is the daughter of
(a) Pandit Deep Chand
(b) Jagdish Prakash
(c) Ustad Bismillah Khan
(d) Pandit ram Chand

58 Who among the following has been appointed the new U.S. Ambassador to India?
(a) Robert Zoellick
(b) Richard Blackwill
(c) Robert Blackwill
(d) Condoleeza Rice

59 Who among the following was in the news in March 2001 who, partnering with Joseph Barbera, created cartoon characters - Fred Flinstone, Yogi Bear and Tom & Jerry?
(a) William Gabriel
(b) Nicholas Stern
(c) William Hanna
(d) Nicholas Ingram

60 Who among the following heads the commission of inquiry to probe the @tehelka.com expose on graft in defence deals?
(a) Justice P. N. Bhagwati
(b) Justice M. S. Verma
(c) Justice Shyam Sunder
(d) Justice K. Venkataswami

61 Which of the following Australian cricketers is nick-named as 'Tugga'?
(a) Mark Waugh

(b) Steve Waugh
(c) Adam Gilchrist
(d) Andrew Symonds

62 Who among the following is the author of the book 'Fury'?
(a) V. S. Naipaul
(b) M. K. Kenon
(c) Vikram Seth
(d) Salman Rushdie

63 At the 73rd Annual Academy Awards in Los Angeles, who among the following won the Oscar for Best Actress?
(a) Marcia Gay Harden
(b) Julia Roberts
(c) Ellen Busryn
(d) Julia Harden

64 Two of India's women weightlifters, Kunjarani Devi (5th) and Kamam Malleswari (13th), have been included in the International Weightlifting Federation's list of 50 Greatest Women Medal Winners of the century. Who among the following heads this list?
(a) Urrulia Maria Isabela (Columbia)
(b) Trefendafilova Milne (Bulgaria)
(c) Maria Takacs (Hungary)
(d) Chen Shu-Chih (Taipei)

65. At the 48th National Film Awards, who among the following received the Best Actor Award?
(a) Anil Kapoor
(b) Shah Rukh Khan
(c) Sanjay Dutt
(d) Hrithik Roshan

66 The first flight of India's GSLV failed to take off on March 28, 2001. It was to ferry which experimental satellite in space?
(a) GSAT - 1
(b) GSAT - 2
(c) PSAT - 1
(d) PSAT - 2

67 Who among the following was the Chief of Lashkar-e-Taiba in Kashmir, who was shot dead in an encounter in Nowgam, Budgam in Central Kashmir on March 28, 2001?

(a) Prof. Hafiz Mohammad Sateed
(b) Salahuddin
(c) Jalauddin
(d) Prof. J. Mohammad

68 Two members of the Jury for selection of 48th National Film Awards resigned while one walked out in protest against the 'rigging' of the awards during March 2001. Who among the following is not one of them?
(a) Madhumita Raut
(b) Shashi Anand
(c) Dhritiman Chaterjee
(d) Pradip Kishen

69 'Operation Trishna' is launched by which of the following State governments?
(a) Rajasthan
(b) Andhra Pradesh
(c) Orissa
(d) Chatisgarh

70 Of the 53 members of Organisation of African Unity, 35 member-countries have ratified the treaty for a 'United States of Africa'. The idea United States of Africa was first floated in 1999 by:
(a) Muammar Gaddafi
(b) Fernando De La Rua
(c) Thabo Mbeki
(d) Nelson Mandela

71 Which among the following is the name of the educational TV channel promoted by the Indira Gandhi National Open University?
(a) Gyan Darshan
(b) Gyan Shikha
(c) Gyan Kund
(d) Gyan Deep

72 Who among the following is the recepient of the newly introduced Inayat Khan Memorial award in 2001?
(a) Ali Akbar Khan
(b) Kishan Maharaj
(c) Vilayat Khan
(d) Bismillah Khan

73 Who among the following is the present coach of Indian Football team?
(a) Noel Wilson
(b) I. M. Vijayan
(c) Suhkwinder Singh
(d) Rajender Singh

74 Parnita Grewal is associated with which of the following games/ sports?
(a) Golf
(b) Athletics
(c) Badminton
(d) Basketball

75 India's first gold refinery, 'Agee Gold Refinery' has been set up at:
(a) Shirpur (Maharashtra)
(b) Andiyur (Tamil Nadu)
(c) Akalkot (Maharahtra)
(d) Kutru (M.P.)

76 Mr. B. P. Verma was in the news during March-April 2001 when CBI registered a corruption case against him. At that time he was the Chairman of :
(a) Press Council of India
(b) Central Board of Excise and Customs
(c) Insurance Regulatory Authority
(d) Enforcement Directorate

77 Who among the following is the Chairman of the Indian Council of Social Science Research who was in the news during April 2001 for seeking Prime Minister's internebtion to save the institute?
(a) Prof. K. L. Mishra
(b) Prof. J. N. Mishra
(c) Prof. H. L. Gupta
(d) Prof. M. L. Sondhi

78 World Sanskrit Conference was held during April 2001 in:
(a) New Delhi
(b) Kathmandu
(c) Port Louis
(d) Mumbai

79 With reference to the 2001 Securities Scam, Madhavpura Mercantile

Co-operative Bank was in the news during March-April 2001. Who was the Chairman

(a) Dinesh Pandya
(b) Ketan Parikh
(c) Ramesh Parikh
(d) Kartikh Parikh

80 Who among the following has not completed the double of 1000 runs and 100 wickets in One-day Internationals?

(a) Sachin Tendulkar
(b) Ravi Shastri
(c) Robin Singh
(d) Prof. M. L. Sondhi

81 To which one of the following Asian cities was the Mughal emperor Bahadur Shah II exiled after India's First War of Independence?

(a) Yangoon
(b) Chittagong
(c) Dhaka
(d) Kabul

82 "Beyond The Last Blue Mountain" is the biography of which of the following famous Indians?

(a) Dhirubhai Ambani
(b) J. R. D. Tata
(c) Zakir Hussain
(d) Sam Pitroda

83 Who among the following Englishmen presided over the 1910 annual session of Congress held in Calcutta?

(a) Sir Henry McMohan
(b) Sir William Wedderburn
(c) Sir Cyril Redcliffe
(d) Ramsay McDonald

84 Who among rhe following is considered as the 'God of Medicine' by practitioners of Ayurveda?

(a) Sushruta
(b) Dhavantri
(c) Charaka
(d) Aryabhatta

85 Himalayan foothills are commonly known as:

(a) Aravallis
(b) Himadri
(c) Himachali
(d) Shivalliks

86 Which of the following is the full form of the 'HAM', a radio operation network, which was in the news during the Gujrat Earthquake relief operations in January 2001?
(a) Hertz, Armstrong, Marconi
(b) High-frequency, Audio, Modulator
(c) Hertz, Armstron, Modulator
(d) Hertz, Aerial, Marconi

87 Who among the following is the President of the Table Tennis Federation of India?
(a) Suresh Prabhu
(b) Ajay Singh Chautala
(c) Probir Moitra
(d) Vipul Mitra

88 Which of the following was the US nuclear-powered submarine that collided with a Japanese trawler south-west of Honolulu in February 2001?
(a) USS Destiny
(b) USS Greenville
(c) USS Fondran
(d) USS Redeville

89 According to the new findings of the human genome research unveiled in February 2001, scientists say that the total number of geneses in human body is between
(a) 30,000 to 40,000
(b) 41,000 to 60,000
(c) 61,000 to 80,000
(d) 81,000 to 100,000

90 Who among the following was bestowed the 'Honorary Knight Commander of the Order of the British Queen' in recognition of his services to music?
(a) Ustad Amjad Ali Khan
(b) Pandit Ravi Shankar
(c) Pandit Shiv Shankar
(d) Zubin Mehta

91 With which of the following companies ONGC Videsh finalised a deal in February 2001, with a 20 percent stake in the giant Sakhalin-1 oil field where production is expected to start in the year 2005?
(a) Hoedeo (Japan)
(b) Sodeco (Japan)
(c) Rosneft (Russia)
(d) Hesneft (Russia)

92 The 25th Senior national Women's Football Championship for S. R. Zaidi Trophy was held in which of the folowing States during February 2001?
(a) Bihar
(b) Orissa
(c) Madhya Pradesh
(d) Karnataka

93 Who among the following is the Chief Executive Officer (acting) of the Prasar Bharti?
(a) Rajiv Ratan Shah
(b) N. K. Sinha
(c) Anil Baijal
(d) D. P. Sandhokar

94 'Gana Shastha' or Public Health Service, which was in the news during the relief operation of quake-ravaged Gujrat, in January 2001, is from which of the following countries?
(a) Sri Lanka
(b) Nepal
(c) Bangladesh
(d) Pakistan

95 The country's first-ever corporatised port, inaugurated by Prime Minister, Mr. Atal Bihari Vajpayee on February 1, 2001, is located at which of the following places?
(a) Ennore
(b) Janput
(c) Udankudi
(d) Mamalipuram

96 Ibrahim Rahimatollah Challange Cup is associated with which of the following games/sports?
(a) Tennis

(b) Football
(c) Badminton
(d) Hockey

97 Who among the following won the Women's Singles title in the Senior National Badminton Championship held in Jaipur on February 7, 2001?
(a) Aparna Popat
(b) Jwalas Gutta
(c) Manjusha Kanwar
(d) Shruti Kurien

98 Who among the following is the new President of the Philippines?
(a) Jose Miguel Arroyo
(b) Gloria Macapagal Arroyo
(c) Joseph Estrada
(d) Mireya Moscoso

99 A collaborative e-book titled 'The Morive' is written by:
(a) Naresh Gupta
(b) Bruce Chizen
(c) Tara Deshpande
(d) Dhirendra Kumar

100 2001 has been declared as the Year of:
(a) Women's Empowerment
(b) Men's Empowerment
(c) Girl Child
(d) Poverty Eradication

101 Who among the following has not been selected for 'Padma Vibhushan' awards announced on the eve of Republic Day 2001?
(a) Zubin Mehta
(b) Hrishikesh Mukherjee
(c) B. R. Chopra
(d) John Kenneth Galbraith

102 Who among the following was the Chief Guest at the 52nd Republic Day celebrations in New Delhi on January 26, 2001?
(a) Abdelaziz Bouteflika
(b) Fernando De La Rua
(c) Maumoon Abdul gayoom
(d) Bashar Al-Assad

103 Who among the following is the Director of the Pakistan's Human Rights Commission who visited India during IPI World Congress in January 2001?

(a) Khwaja Sharif
(b) I. A. Rehman
(c) Kamila Hayat
(d) M. Abdul Aziz

104 The earthquake which rocked Gujrat during January 2001 had its epicentre at:

(a) 20 km north-west of Bhuj in Rann of Kutch
(b) 20 km south-west of Bhuj in Rann of Kutch
(c) 20 km north-east of Bhuj in Rann of Kutch
(d) 20 km north-west of Palanpur in Rann of Kutch

105 Who among the following is the President of All India Muslim Personal law Board (AIMPLB)?

(a) Maulana Qazi Mujahidul Islam Qasmi
(b) Maulana Nizamuddin Yusuf H. Muchhala
(c) Maulana Sajid Nomani
(d) Maulana Zafaryab Jilani

106 Which of the following companies was not among the winners of Golden Peacock National Quality Awards presented in January 2001, during the inauguration cermony of the 11th World Congress on Total Quality 2001?

(a) Reliance Industries Ltd.
(b) Wipro Infotech
(c) Bharat Petroleum
(d) Infosys Technologies

107 In which of the following cities, the annual meeting of the World Economic Forum was held during January 2001?

(a) Vienna
(b) Davos
(c) Lyons
(d) Madrid

108 At rhe 58th Annual Golden Globe Awards in January 2001, who among the following won the Best Director Award?

(a) Ang Lee
(b) Stephen Gaghan

(c) Robert Downey
(d) Beniclo Del Toro

109 During January 2001, World bank announced a $180 million loan project for which of the following States?
(a) Andhra Pradesh
(b) Maharashtra
(c) Rajsthan
(d) Punjab

110 The Popocatepeti volcano, which shot a plume of ash and smoke more than eight kms high during December 2000-January 2001, is in which of the following countries?
(a) U.S.A.
(b) Japan
(c) Italy
(d) Mexico

111 Who among the following is the President of BJP?
(a) Bangaru Laxman
(b) Jana Krishnamurthi
(c) G.M.C. Balyogi
(d) Brajesh Mishra

112 Indian National Congress held its first session at
(a) Calcutta
(b) Madras
(c) Bombay
(d) Poona

113 The Rathas at Mahabalipuram are
(a) Square or Rectangular
(b) Monolithic Structure
(c) Eight in number
(d) All of the above

114 The boundary between India and pakistan was demarketed by
(a) Lord Mountbatten
(b) Sir Cyril Radcliffe
(c) Sir Stafford Cripps
(d) Pethic Lawrence

115 Name the scholor who visited India along with Mahmud of Ghazni?
(a) Ibn-Batutah

(b) Al-Beruni
(c) Al-Firdausi
(d) Al-Razi

116 Which one of the following is the earliest school of Indian philosphy?
(a) Samkhya
(b) Yoga
(c) Vaisesika
(d) Karma mimamsa

117 "Vande Matram" was first published in
(a) Kesari
(b) Gitanjali
(c) Harijan
(d) Anandmath

118 The famous 'Vale of kashmir' refers to:
(a) A longitudinal valley in the Himalayas
(b) A valley occupying an anticline on the back of a nappe
(c) A valley which had been a lake till the Pleistocene
(d) All of the above

119 Who among the following is the U.S. Secretary of States?
(a) William Cohen
(b) Colin Powell
(c) Madeleine albright
(d) Janet Reno

120 An observer at a point on the earth, where only the penumbra region of moon's shadow will move past, will observe a
(a) Partial solar eclipse
(b) Partial lunar eclipse
(c) Total solar eclipse
(d) Total lunar eclipse

121 Loams are formed where the soils have equal proportion of:
(a) Silt and clay
(b) Clay and sand
(c) Sand and silt
(d) Sand, silt and clay

122 Main river in Sikkim is
(a) Jaldhaka

(b) Manas
(c) Tista
(d) Torsa

123 Merit goods are those goods
(a) Which are available at concessional rates
(b) Which are short in supply
(c) The consumption of which adds to the national income
(d) The consumption of which benefits the non-consumer also

124 Match the following

Energy	Operating process
(P) Kinetic	(1) River, wind, wave, gravitation
(Q) Heat	(2) Hot, spring, valcano
(R) Radiant	(3) Aurora, lighting
(S) Electrical	(4) Solar insolation

	P	Q	R	S
(A)	1	2	3	4
(B)	2	1	4	3
(C)	1	2	4	3
(D)	4	3	2	1

125 The lines joining the places of equal labour and transportation costs are known as
(a) Isotims
(b) Isochrones
(c) Isohypses
(d) Isodapanes

126 Which one of the following canals is not used for irrigation?
(a) Upper Ganga Canal
(b) Indira Gandhi Canal
(c) Western Yamuna Canal
(d) Buckingham Canal

127 Which forest belt supplies most of the world's requirement of newsprint?
(a) Tropical Deciduous
(b) Tropical Evergreen
(c) Coniferous
(d) Mediterranean

128 A subscriber to the new issues expecting to sell his allotment of

securities at a profit, when trading begins, is called a
(a) Bull
(b) Bear
(c) Stag
(d) Cow

129 Who among the following is the President of the National Consumer Disputes Redressal Commission (NCDRC)
(a) Justice B. P. Jeevan Reddy
(b) Justice Shyam Sunder
(c) Justice Mohammed Shamim
(d) Justice D. P. Wadhwa

130 'Foreign aid' to India denotes inflow of resources from abroad in the form of
(a) Credit extended by the suppliers
(b) NRI deposits
(c) Grants and grant component of loans
(d) Grants and loans

131 Rupee convertability aims at
(a) Increasing of exports
(b) Reducing bureaucratic control
(c) Decreasing incentive for Havala market
(d) All of the above

132 In India, "budgetary deficit" of the Government of India (GOI) is defined as the
(a) Net increase in the GOI treasury bill and withdrawls from cash
(b) Net addition to total liabilities of the GOI
(c) Net increase in RBI credit to the GOI
(d) Excess of revenue expenditure over revenue receipt of the GOI

133 Total Revenue of a firm is maximum when Marginal Revenue
(a) Is greater than zero
(b) Becomes zero
(c) Becomes negative
(d) None of these

134 Currency notes of RBI must be backed by not less than a specified
(a) Percentage of note issue in the form of gold and foreign securities

(b) Percentage of note issue in form government securities
(c) Amount of gold and foreign securities
(d) Amount of government securities

135 A Free Port is one which
(a) Allows duty-free imports
(b) Does not have customs checking
(c) Has free entry of re-exportable goods
(d) Has free entry of imports from specified countries

136 The exchange value of the rupee is determined with reference to
(a) The US dollor
(b) The British pound
(c) A basket of selected currencies
(d) None of the above

137 Under perfect competetion and short run, a firm would continue to produce, provide
(a) It is able to recover its fixed costs
(b) It is able to recover its variable costs
(c) Its loss does not exceed a specified amount
(d) It is able to recover its total cost

138 The economic growth during the year 2000-2001 is
(a) 6.4%
(b) 6.2%
(c) 6%
(d) 5.8%

139 The UN Secretary-General, Mr. Kofi Annan, visited India in
(a) March, 2001
(b) January 2001
(c) December 2000
(d) October 2000

140 Which of the following is not an organ of the U.N.O.?
(a) International Labour Organisation
(b) International Court of Justice
(c) Security Council
(d) Economic and Social Council

141 The State of Jammu and Kashmir adopted its seperate Constitution on
(a) January 26, 1950

(b) August 15, 1952
(c) November 26, 1957
(d) January 26, 1957

142 "Revenue receipts" of the Government of India do not include
(a) Interest
(b) Profits and Dividends
(c) Recoveries and Loans
(d) Rent from properties

143 Which one of the following is a State subject included in the State List Only?
(a) Education
(b) Fisheries
(c) Forest
(d) Railways

144 In which Schedule of the Constitution are the land reforms laws included
(a) Seventh
(b) Eight
(c) Ninth
(d) Tenth

145 Equal pay for equal work for both men and women has been laid down in the Indian Constitution as one of the
(a) Fundamental Rights
(b) Fundamental Duties
(c) Guidelines in the Preamble
(d) Directive Principles of State Policy

146 For amendment of the election procedure of the President of India or his powers, the requirement is that
(a) The Parliament pases the bill with 2/3 majority
(b) No amendment is passed when a person holds the office
(c) Besides passage of the bill in Parliament by required majority, the legislatures of at least half of the States must ratify
(d) Two third majority in Rajya Sabha is necessary

147 Who among the following is the Foreign Secretary?
(a) T. R. Prassad
(b) Yogendra Narain
(c) Chokila Iyer

(d) Ajit Kumar

148 In which of the following matters, the Rajya Sabha has co-equal powers with the Lok Sabha?

(a) Power to initiate the Budget
(b) Power to pass the Finance Bill
(c) Power to adopt motion of noconfidence against the government
(d) Power to amend the Constitution

149 When a piece of Iron is dipped in concentrated nitric acid, the iron becomes

(a) Chemically inert
(b) Chemically more active
(c) Hard and brittle
(d) Soft

150 Which one of the following materials is used for absorbing neutrons in a nuclear reactor?

(a) Lead
(b) Zinc
(c) Uranium
(d) Cadmium

151 Consider the following statements:

(i) For altering the boundaries of the States, the Constitution needs to be amended

(ii) The above amendment must be retified by more than half of all the States in India.

(a) Both the statements are wrong
(b) Statement (i) is wrong but (ii) is correct
(c) Statement (ii) is wrong but (i) is correct
(d) Both the statements are correct

152 The name of a candidate for the office of the President of India may be proposed by

(a) Any five citizen of India
(b) Any one member of the Electrol College
(c) Any five members of the Parliament
(d) Any ten members of the Electrol College

153 Which of the following is not obtain from green leafy vegitables

(a) Vitamin A
(b) Vitamin B (Thiamine)

(c) Folic Acid
(d) Pentothenic Acid

154 Velocity of light is
(a) Constant
(b) Directly proportional to wavelength
(c) Inversely propotional to wavelength
(d) Dependent on frequency

155 Sun's energy is produced by
(a) Nuclear fission
(b) Nuclear fusion
(c) Burning of Gases
(d) None of these

156 A common weed *Catharanthus roseus* (Sadabahar) is the source of medicine used in the treatment of
(a) Leukemia
(b) Gout
(c) Coronary heart disease
(d) Poliomylitis

157 If the length of the filament in an electric bulb is reduced, the latter will glow with intensity that is
(a) Low
(b) Medium
(c) More
(d) Normal as in original

158 A specific test for detection of tuberculosis is
(a) Widal's
(b) Mantoux's
(c) Kahn's
(d) Robert's

159 All the ecosystems taken togather in a geographical area from a bigger unit called
(a) Community
(b) Territory
(c) Biome
(d) Biosphere

160 The crop most susceptible to frost is
(a) Cotton

(b) Wheat
(c) Red gram
(d) Black gram

161 Which of the following is false?
(a) the genetic information machinery is similar in bacteria and man
(b) All organisms are related through ancestry
(c) Divers kind of organisms are evolved at various periods of time hence their basic life processes are different
(d) Microbes, plants and animals appear so distinct from one another that they cannot have similarities in patterns of reproduction

162 The greatest cricketer Sir Donald Bradman passed away on February 26, 2001. He belonged to
(a) Australia
(b) England
(c) New Zealand
(d) South Africa

163 A pendulum clock will run faster at which of the following places than other
(a) On a mountain
(b) Sea shore
(c) 20th floor of building
(d) Mine

164 Who was the Congress President when India became free?
(a) Mahatma Gandhi
(b) Jawahar Lal Nehru
(c) Sardar Patel
(d) J. B. Kriplani

165 The Simon Commission visited India to
(a) See the imprtant historical places
(b) Discuss the demand for the formation of Pakistan
(c) Enquire into the progress of responsible government in India
(d) None of the above

166 Who was the Prime Minister of England at the time of grant of Independence to India?
(a) Nevilloe Chaberian

(b) Winston Churchill
(c) Clement Attlee
(d) Lord Home

167 Who was the head of the committee formed by the government to enquire into the Jallianwallah Bagh massacre?
(a) O. Dyer
(b) General Dyer
(c) John Simon
(d) Hunter

168 Which of the following movements truly reflected the spireit of Hindu-Muslim unity?
(a) Swadeshi movement
(b) Civil Disobedience Movement
(c) Quit India Movement
(d) Khilafat Movement

169 At present how many SAARC countries have women Prime Ministers?
(a) One
(b) Two
(c) Three
(d) None

170 The present Prime Minister of Nepal is
(a) K. P. Bhattarai
(b) Manmohan Adhikari
(c) Pawan Kumar Chamling
(d) Girja Prassad Koirala

171 Holding of elections for the Village Panchayat is decided by the
(a) Collector
(b) Election Commission
(c) Central Government
(d) State Government

172 What did Gandhiji do to practise the ideals of truth and non-violence in 1916?
(a) He joined the Indian National Congress
(b) He founded Sabarmati ashram near Ahmedabad
(c) He founded the Gujrat Vidyapeeth
(d) He started an All-India Satyagraha

173 In the Bangkok Asian games, held in December 1998, the countries which secured the first and second positions in winning the maximun number of Gold Medals were

	First Position	*Second Position*
(a)	South Korea	Japan
(b)	China	South Korea
(c)	China	Japan
(d)	South Korea	China

174 "Against the Grain" is the title of the autobiography of
(a) R. Venkatraman
(b) Boris Yeltsin
(c) John Major
(d) Benazir Bhutto

175 Where is the Santosh Power Project
(a) Nepal
(b) Bhutan
(c) Sikkim
(d) Arunanchal Pradesh

176 The maximum temperature that the human skin can tolerate without getting blisters is
(a) 40ºC
(b) 60ºC
(c) 80ºC
(d) 100ºC

177 Who is the recipient of the Jnanpith Award for 1999?
(a) Girish Karnard
(b) Sitakanta Mahapatra
(c) Nirmal Verma
(d) Dharmvir Bharti

178 Who among the following is/are recipient(s) of the 2000 Nobel Prize for Peace?
(a) John Hume
(b) David Trimble
(c) Kim Dae-Jung
(d) None of these

179 India House is located in
(a) London

(b) New Delhi
(c) Mumbai
(d) Kolkata

180 Most of the 2001 Oscar Awards were bagged by the film
(a) Jurasic Park
(b) Gladiator
(c) The Piano
(d) My Concubine

181 The fragmented remains of Comet Shoemaker-Levy 9 hit the outer surface of which of the following planet?
(a) Jupiter
(b) Venus
(c) Mars
(d) Mercury

182 Who among the following is a recipient of the Gandhi Peace Prize for 1999?
(a) Ramakrishna Mission
(b) Sunderilal Bahuguna
(c) Baba Amte
(d) M. G. K. Menon

183 Which of the following countries did not participate in World Cup '99 held in England in May/June 1999?
(a) Kenya
(b) Scotland
(c) Holland
(d) All of these

184 The Organistion of Islamic Conference, set up in May 1971, has a membership of
(a) 30 countries
(b) 25 countries
(c) 45 countries
(d) 54 countries

185 The Presidential refernce of the Ayodhya issue to the Supreme Court for opinion was made under
(a) Article 143 (1)
(b) Article 138 (1)
(c) Article 138 (2)

(d) None of these

186 Indian sepoys in the Bengal Army revolted because
(a) The British officers ill treated them
(b) The British tried to make them use the greased cartridge
(c) The British discountinued the payment of the field allowance
(d) The Bristish passed the General Service Enlistment Act.

187 The important feature of shifting cultivation is
(a) Change of cultivation site
(b) Rotation of crops
(c) Cultivation by transplantation
(d) Cultivation of leguminous crops

188 How many countries participated in the International Fleet Review held in Mumbai in February 2001?
(a) 23
(b) 17
(c) 29
(d) 30

189 'Socialist pattern of economic development' is associated with the plans of
(a) Russia
(b) China
(c) India
(d) U.S.A.

190 An economy is at the 'take off ' stage on its path to development when it
(a) Becomes stagnant
(b) Begins steady growth
(c) Is liberised
(d) Gets maximum foreign aid

191 Credit is a
(a) Stock concept
(b) Flow concept
(c) A stock-flow concept
(d) None of the above

192 Mathura refinary receives crude oil from
(a) Cauvery basin
(b) Vadodara

(c) Kandla
(d) None of these

193 *Assertion A:* Humayun was himself responsible for his misfortunes
Reasoning R: He became jealous of his brother
(a) Both A and R are true and R is the correct explanation of A
(b) Both A and R are true but R is not correct explanation of A
(c) A is true but R is wrong
(d) Both A and R are wrong

194 Which one of the following rivers is not tributary of Ganga?
(a) Indrawati
(b) Son
(c) Gomati
(d) Yamuna

195 The Gol Gumbaz at Bijapur is a
(a) Mosque
(b) Tomb
(c) Palace
(d) College

196 Which of the following is not a unit of time?
(a) Light Year
(b) Nano Second
(c) Micro Second
(d) Second

197 Which of the Harappan sites had dock?
(a) Mohenjodaro
(b) Harappa
(c) Lothal
(d) Alamgirpur

198 Who among the following Sultans of Delhi has been described by historians as the 'mixture of opposits'?
(a) Balban
(b) Alauddin Khilji
(c) Muhamad Tuglaq
(d) Ibrahim Lodi

199 Who among the following rulers held a religious asembly at Prayag every five years?
(a) Ashoka

(b) Kanishka
(c) Chandra Gupta Vikramaditya
(d) Harshavardhana

200 Match the following:

List (i) (Quantity)	*List (ii) (Unit)*
1 Electric Force	(a) Volt between two charged bodies
2 Electric Charge	(b) Newton
3 Electric Potential	(c) Farad

(a) 1 _____ d 2 _____ b 3 _____ c 4 _____ a
(b) 1 _____ c 2 _____ a 3 _____ b 4 _____ d
(c) 1 _____ a 2 _____ c 3 _____ d 4 _____ b

201 The red colour of ripe tomatoes is due to the presence of:
(a) Chlorophyll
(b) Carotenoids
(c) Vitamins
(d) Harmones

202 Swarajya was declared as the goal of the Congress at its session held in 1906 at:
(a) Bombay
(b) Calcutta
(c) Lucknow
(d) Madras

203 'Harry potter and the prisoner of Azkaban' was written by:
(a) Jarie Austen
(b) R. K. Rowling
(c) J. R. R. Tolkien
(d) James Patterson

204 Non-stick cooking utensils are coated with:
(a) Black Paint
(b) Polyethylene
(c) Polystyrene
(d) Teflon

205 The Ozone layer in the upper part of the atmosphere protects us from:
(a) Infra-red rays
(b) Visible radiations
(c) Ultraviolet radiations

(d) Cosmic rays

206 Deodorant used in toilets contains:
(a) Benzole
(b) Benzyne
(c) Phthalic acid
(d) None of these

207 Sunlight provides:
(a) Vitamin A to the body
(b) Vitamin B to the body
(c) Vitamin C to the body
(d) Vitamin D to the body

208 Human body needs a constant supply of proteins to survive. the first part of the digestive system to begin digesting proteins is:
(a) Mouth
(b) Stomach
(c) Small Intestines
(d) Large Intestines

209 The Legislatiive Council in a State may be created or abolished by the:
(a) President on the recommendation of the Governor
(b) Parliament
(c) Parliament after the State Legislative Assembly passes a resolution to that effect
(d) Governor on a recommendation by the state cabinet

210 Who among the following won the Wimbledon Championships five times in a row?
(a) Pete Sampras
(b) Bjorn Borg
(c) Rod Laver
(d) John Newcombe

211 Asia's biggest garbage cum organic fertilizer factory is being set up at:
(a) Thiruvananthpuram
(b) Mysore
(c) Calcutta
(d) Hyderabad
(e) None of these

212 During the UN Millenium Summit, India has signed an International Convention initiated by ____ to stop finance of international terrorism
(a) Russia
(b) France
(c) Zambia
(d) USA
(e) Germany

213 From 1st October onwards, OPEC agreed to raise oil supplies by ____ barrels a day to stop the rise in crude prices
(a) 80,000
(b) 800,000
(c) 8,000,000
(d) 8,000
(e) 800

214 Buddhdeb Das Gupta won the Special Director's Award for his film ____ at Venice film festival
(a) Vanaprastham
(b) Malli
(c) Uttara
(d) The Terrorist
(e) Asht Nayika

215 Which of the following Articles of Indian Constitution clearly States:
"Election to the House of the People to the legislative asembly of States to be on the basis of adult suffrage."
(a) 102
(b) 326
(c) 224
(d) 84
(e) 325

216 British safety council has given safety award, 1999 to ____. The award is also known as the Oscar in the field of industrial safety.
(a) NTPC Rihand Super Thermal Power Project
(b) NTPC Jhaptha Project
(c) BHEL
(d) Bongaigaon Refinery
(e) Mathura Refinery

217 Dr. Surinder K. Vasal and Dr. Evangelina Villages, have been jointly awarded the:

(a) WHO prize
(b) World food prize
(c) Nobel prize
(d) UN prize
(e) UNESCO prize

218 India has recently repaid Rs ____ crore of external debt for the first time after independence.

(a) 27,000
(b) 26,000
(c) 20,000
(d) 35,000
(e) 50,000

219 From 16th-20th September, 2000, Auto-fair-2000 is being organised at ____ .

(a) Kerala, Kochi
(b) Bangalore
(c) Chennai
(d) Mumbai
(e) New Delhi

220 Name the country, calling for a promotion of a multipolar international configuration with a view to promote peace and regional development:

(a) Japan
(b) China
(c) Russia
(d) France
(e) Germany

221 Which of the following trade union called off the Telecom strike, prior to others?

(a) Federation of National Telecom Organisation
(b) National Federation of Telecom Employees
(c) Bhartiya Telecom Employees Federation
(d) Bharat Sanchar Karamchari Sangh
(e) None of these

222 Which of the political parties was derecognised by the Election

Commissioner as a State party on the basis of its performance in the Lok Sabha and assembly polls in 1999:
(a) Rashtriya Kranti Dal
(b) Trinamool Congress
(c) Samta Party
(d) Lik Shakti
(e) All of these

223 Roy Frederich was the player associated with which game?
(a) Golf
(b) Cricket
(c) Swimming
(d) Chess
(e) Hockey

224 In the 55th UN General Assembly, which country became the 189th member of the UN?
(a) North Korea
(b) Kiribati
(c) Tuvalu
(d) East Timor
(e) Zambia

225 Mr. Kamaluddin Ahmed has been appointed as the new member of:
(a) Finance Commission
(b) National Council of Applied Economic Research
(c) Union Cabinet Committee
(d) Disinvestment Commission
(e) Planning Commission

226 Since 1969 at London, Wisdon Trophy has been lifted for the first time by ____ defeating West Indies.
(a) India
(b) Sri Lanka
(c) Pakistan
(d) England
(e) Bangladesh

227 Dr. Gro-Herlem Brundtland is the Director General of ____
(a) WHO
(b) FAO

(c) UNEP
(d) UNICEF
(e) UNDP

228 Indian Oil Corporation is going to buy 74.46% government's stake in:
(a) Bongaigaon refinery
(b) Chennai refinary
(c) Numaligarh refinary
(d) Cochin refinary
(e) Panipat refinary

229 Which of the following statement is/are not true:
(a) Justice Balakrishna Eradi Commission was set up on insolvancy law.
(b) The commission recommended the repeal of Sick Industrial Companies Act.
(c) The commission wanted winding up of the Board for Industrial and Financial Reconstruction and the Appellate Authority for Industrial and Financial Reconstruction.
(d) The committee has suggested setting up of a National Tribunal with jurisdiction and powers of the company law board.
(e) The commission wants an autonomous body for industrial development.

230 In the 2nd round of US open tennis championship Andre Agassi was defeated by:
(a) Arnauld Clement
(b) Pete sampras
(c) Marat Safin
(d) Jerad Palmer
(e) None of these

231 The tallest tree of the world is in India, at Japfu mountain range in:
(a) Assam
(b) Manipur
(c) Mizoram
(d) Nagaland
(e) Sikkim

232 Which of the following statements is/are false?
(a) Al-Aqsa mosque is in Jerusalem.

(b) It is the third holiest site in Islam.
(c) Jewish community want a free entry in this area but Islamic community is opposing the dicision.
(d) They are the heart of dispute between Israel and Palestine.
(e) Western wall near it is a holy place for Christian.

233 Franz Harary is associated with which field?
(a) Illusionist
(b) Literature
(c) Cartoonist
(d) Acting
(e) Sport

234 The youngest Indian Olympic participant in Sydney Olympic is:
(a) K. Humpy
(b) Abhinav Bindra
(c) Aparna Popat
(d) P. Gopichand
(e) Mahesh Bhupati

235 Who created the record by clocking 3 : 45 : 12 hours in crossing 30 km distance between Tarifa and Morocco *i.e.* Strait of Gibralter?
(a) Nisha Millet
(b) Bula Chaudhary
(c) Arti Shah
(d) Both (a) and (b)
(e) None of these

236 Which of these guidlines is/are false for opening STD?
(a) One-time entry fee of Rs. 100 crore.
(b) Operator would have to give a bank guarantee of Rs. 400 crore.
(c) In the 1st phase operator would have to cover 15% of the prescribed area in 2 years faling which the bank guarantee worth Rs. 100 crore would be forefeited.
(d) Paid up capital at Rs. 500 crore
(e) Foreign equity cap is at 49 percent.

237 Match the following:
A. 73rd Amendment Bill
B. 90th Amendment Bill
C. 85th Amendment Bill
D. 87th Amendment Bill

E. 89th Amendment Bill

(i) seeks to devolve 29 per cent of Central taxes to the states.

(ii) seeks todo away with direct elections mandatory to only the lowest tiers, the gram panchayats, and optional to the block and district panchayats.

(iii) deals with the reservation of 33% of seats for women in the Parliament.

(iv) reintroduces the panchayti raj system for the village assembly of the gram sabha.

(v) deals woth filling up of 50 percent reservation on current as well as backlog vacancies and for discontinution of the special recruitment drive.

Codes:

	A	B	C	D	E
(a)	(v)	(iv)	(iii)	(i)	(ii)
(b)	(iv)	(v)	(iii)	(ii)	(i)
(c)	(i)	(ii)	(iii)	(iv)	(v)
(d)	(v)	(iv)	(iii)	(ii)	(i)
(e)	(i)	(iii)	(ii)	(v)	(iv)

238 Dabur group is going to tie up with:
(a) All State Insurance Company
(b) Royal Sun Alliance
(c) ING Insurance
(d) Canada Life
(e) Allianz AG

239 On 30th June 2000, the government reduced, with restropective effect from effect from 1st April 2000, the interst rate on Employees Provident Fund savings to 11 percent from 12 percent. Total deposits under the EPF scheme are around Rs _____crore.
(a) 50,000
(b) 60,000
(c) 70,000
(d) 80,000
(e) None of these

240 On 8th September 2000, oil prices were highest as compared to the last 10 years' oil prices. The prices were:
(a) $ 38 per barrel
(b) $ 37 per barrel

(c) $ 35 per barrel
(d) $ 40 per barrel
(e) $ 28 per barrel

241 India's Ambassador and permanent representative to the UN Conference on Disarmament in Geneva is:
(a) Anil Baijal
(b) Rakesh Sood
(c) B. P. Singh
(d) Alok Prassad
(e) Vibhu Man Singh

242 Hubble telescope completed 10 years in space on:
(a) 21st April 2000
(b) 8th September 2000
(c) 24th April 2000
(d) 24th September 2000
(e) None of these

243 Indias biggest optical telescope is being set up at:
(a) Devasthal park in Nainital
(b) Devasthal peak in Nainital
(c) China top in Nainital
(d) Bhimtal in Nainital
(e) Sat Tal in Nainital

244 ASCI white, the fastest super computer in the world belongs to _____ family.
(a) Microsoft
(b) IBM
(c) Wipro
(d) Satyam
(e) Apple

245 1st company from India, to be listed on the Chicago Board Options Exchange is:
(a) Wipro
(b) Satyam Infoway
(c) Reliance
(d) Tata
(e) Raymonds

246 Discovery of God is a book written by:

(a) Khushwant Singh
(b) Anjali Ela Menon
(c) Amitav Ghosh
(d) Rafiq Zakaria
(e) Amit Choudhary

247 'Golden hours' is a name of:
(a) free e-mail service
(b) technical online service by Satyam
(c) Programme to be telecasred on Zee TV
(d) Programme to be telecasted on DD Metro between 7:00-9:00 p.m.
(e) Special Scheme of Delhi Police

248 Omerta is a novel written by:
(a) Richard Branson
(b) Mario Puzo
(c) Benazir Bhutto
(d) Bapsi Sidhwa
(e) Christopher Anderson

249 Chris Camer is the president of:
(a) Channel 1
(b) CNN International
(c) BBC news network
(d) Star Channel
(e) Sahara T.V.

250 Enterprises India, an international conference was held at _____ in July 2000:
(a) Canberra
(b) Durban
(c) Frankfurt
(d) Okinawa
(e) Calcutta

251 Who was the leader of Bardoli Satyagraha in 1926?
(a) Usha Mehta
(b) Mahatma Gandhi
(c) Sardar Vallabhbhai Patel
(d) Ram Chandra Shukla
(e) All of these

252 In 1906, from Bengal, Birendra Kumar Ghosh and Bhupendranath Dutta, started a newspaper named:
(a) Sandhya
(b) Maharatta
(c) Yavnpriya
(d) Indian Statesman
(e) Yugantar

253 The basin of which of the following river is regarded as having the highest hydal power potential?
(a) Amazon
(b) Congo
(c) Mississippi
(d) Nile
(e) None of these

254 The traditional lands of the Nomads of Central Asia are:
(a) Mongolia and Tibet
(b) Sinkiang and Turkistan
(c) Kirghiz Steppe
(d) All of these
(e) None of these

255 Marino sheep rearing is the predominant pastoral activity in:
(a) Argentina
(b) Australia
(c) Denmark
(d) USA
(e) None of the above

256 Bandipur national park, situated in Karnataka is known for
(a) Tiger
(b) Elephants
(c) Bison
(d) Sloth bear
(e) All of these

257 Velavadar national park, famous for lrge concentration of black-buck is located in:
(a) Rajsthan
(b) Gujrat
(c) Andhra Pradesh

(d) Kerala
(e) Assam

258 Council for Advancement of People's Action and Rural Technology was started on 1st September, in the year:
(a) 1980
(b) 1982
(c) 1984
(d) 1986
(e) 1988

259 Arabica and Robusta are the prominent varieties of:
(a) Tea
(b) Cotton
(c) Silk
(d) Pulses
(e) Coffee

260 When do we observe Commonwealth day?
(a) 24th March
(b) 24th April
(c) 24th May
(d) 24th June
(e) 24th July

261 When was the Dandi March undertaken?
(a) December31, 1929
(b) March 12, 1930
(c) April 5, 1930
(d) May 5, 1930

262 Who was the first propounder of the doctrine of Passive Resistance?
(a) B. G. Tilak
(b) Aurobindo Ghosh
(c) Lajpat Rai
(d) G. K. Gokhale

263 Tricolour was adopted as the national Flag in the
(a) Lahore Congress
(b) Belgaum Congress
(c) Allahabad Congress
(d) Haripura Congress

264 Who was the Congress President during 1940-46?

(a) Jawaharlal Nehru
(b) Sardar Vallabhbhai Patel
(c) Maulana Azad
(d) Rajendra Prassad

265 Who presided over the first session of the Indian National Congress?
(a) A. O. Hume
(b) W. C. Bannerjee
(c) Surendranath Bannerjee
(d) Badruddin Tyabji

266 What for the Morley-Minto Reforms of 1909 are known?
(a) Separate Electorates
(b) Provincial Dyarchy
(c) Provicial Autonomy
(d) Federalism

267 Hanging valley is very common in
(a) High mountains
(b) Sub-arctic region
(c) Glciated areas
(d) Coastal belt

268 Which of the following is correctly matched?

	Wildlife Sanctuary	*State*
(a)	Bandipur	Tamil Nadu
(b)	Manas	Uttar Pradesh
(c)	Ranthambor	Rajsthan
(d)	Simlipal	Bihar

269 Two seas or water-bodies connected by a narrow stretch of water is known as a
(a) Bay
(b) Strait
(c) Paninsula
(d) Isthmus

270 Iron ore from Kudremukh mines is exported from
(a) Marmagao
(b) Cochin
(c) Mangalore
(d) Chennai

271 The largest producer of coffee in the world is

(a) Brazil
(b) Sri Lanka
(c) India
(d) Myanmar

272 The word 'dendritic' is associated with
(a) Wind
(b) Waves
(c) Rivers
(d) Glaciers

273 When the earth is at maximum distance from the sun, it is called
(a) Aphelion
(b) Perihelion
(c) Equinox
(d) Sidereal

274 Mud houses are cooler in summers and warmer in winters as compared to brick houses because
(a) Mud is a good conductor
(b) Mud is a bad conductor
(c) Mud is a poor insultor
(d) Evoporation of water causes cooling in summers and sunlight coming through holes causes warming in winters

275 After long periods of use, a gray spot develops on the inside of a bulb. This is because
(a) The tungsten filament evaporates and collects there
(b) The heat of the bulb scorches the glass at the top
(c) Dust inside the bulb condenses on the top
(d) Glass undergoes a change due to the heat

276 Which of the following types of radiations is absorbed by the upper layer of atmosphere?
(a) Radio-waves
(b) Infrared
(c) Visible
(d) Ultraviolet

277 Ice cubes are added to glass of pure water and a glass pure alcohol. The ice would be
(a) At a higher level of water
(b) At a higher level of Alcohol

(c) At the same level of both
(d) Floating in Alcohol and sinking in water

278 Should cars have bumpers that collapse under impact?
(a) Yes, since the offending car should get damaged and pay for the mistake
(b) No, since it would be very expensive to get repaired
(c) No, since the colliding car would then ram into occupants and kill them
(d) Yes, since they help to absorb the impact of a collision and keep the occupants safe

279 What is the common in AIDS, mumps and poliomyelitis?
(a) Young children get affected most readily
(b) No effective vaccine has yet been developed for them
(c) These are caused by virus
(d) Their germs can be transmitted through blood transfusions

280 Approximately how many times each day do our heart valves open and close normally?
(a) 10,000 times
(b) 1,00,000 times
(c) 1,50,000 times
(d) 2,00,000 times

281 Which of the following enzymes converts protien into peptones?
(a) Pepsin
(b) Trypsin
(c) Erepsin
(d) Enterokinase

282 The deficiency of iron in man may result in
(a) Anaemia
(b) Night blindness
(c) Scurvy
(d) Rickets

283 Protein which renders a cell less susceptible to attack by virus is called
(a) Actomyosin
(b) Chloromycetin
(c) Hybridoma
(d) Inferon

284 Haemophilia is mostly associated with
(a) Labourers
(b) Royal Families
(c) Miners
(d) Sportsmen

285 The Secretary of States for India during British rule was
(a) An official who worked as the Secretary to the Viceroy of India
(b) A Secretary level official appointed in each Presidency of India
(c) A British minister given full control over the Government of India
(d) A senior officer appointed by the Viceroy to look into the internal adminstration in India

286 'Lucknow Pact' was a deal between the
(a) Indians and British about legislative seats
(b) Hindus and the Muslims regarding seat sharing in legislatures
(c) Depressed castes and Brahmins about job reservations
(d) Hindus and Sikhs about job reservations

287 The joint session of the Congress and Muslim League was held in 1916 at
(a) Delhi
(b) Kanpur
(c) Lucknow
(d) Madras

288 Who among the following founded the 'All India Depressed Classes Federation' in 1920?
(a) M. K. Gandhi
(b) Jyotiba Phule
(c) G. K. Gokhle
(d) B. R. Ambedkar

289 The treaty of Versailles humilated
(a) Austria
(b) Germany
(c) England
(d) France

290 Who among the following was not a part of the Mauryan dynasty?
(a) Ajatsatru

(b) Bindusara
(c) Chandragupta Maurya
(d) None of the above

291 When and which Governer-General decided to make English the medium of instruction in India?
(a) 1805-Lord Wellesley
(b) 1845-Lord Hardinge
(c) 1835-Lord William Bentinck
(d) 1850-Lord Dalhousie

292 The first trading centre established by the Bristish was
(a) Calcutta
(b) Surat
(c) Madras
(d) Bombay

293 Who among the following is acknowledged as the pioneer of local self-government in India?
(a) Rippon
(b) Mayo
(c) Lytton
(d) Curzon

294 The Mir Bakshi of the Mughal Emperors was head of
(a) Intelligence
(b) Foreign affairs
(c) Army organisation
(d) Finance

295 Sangam age is associated with the history of
(a) Benaras
(b) Allahabad
(c) Tamil Nadu
(d) Khajuraho

296 Who among the following is popularly known as 'Periyar'?
(a) C. V. Raman Pillai
(b) C. N. Mudaliar
(c) E. V. Ramaswamy Naicker
(d) L. Ramkrishna Pillai

297 In which of the following places was the Ryotwari settlement introduced?

(a) Uttar Pradesh and Punjab
(b) North-West Provinces and Punjab
(c) Madras and Bambay
(d) Bengal and Bihar

298 Normal blood pressure of a man is
(a) 80/120 mm Hg
(b) 90/140 mm Hg
(c) 20/160 mm Hg
(d) 85/150 mm Hg

299 The pigment involved in photosynthetic activity is
(a) Anthocyanin
(b) Fucoxanthin
(c) Carotenoid
(d) Chlorophyll

300 Sugarcane plants are usually propogated by vegetative means because
(a) They donot produce seeds
(b) It is possible to maintain genetic quality
(c) The incidence of disease may be reduced
(d) The seeds are not viable

301 Free-living nitrogen fixing micro-organism are
(a) Rhizobia
(b) Soil fungi
(c) Vesicular arbuscular mycorrhiza
(d) Blue green algae

302 How can a dairy farmer reduce fodder consumption by his cattle and also increase milk production?
(a) By incresing the supply of feed concentrate
(b) By stall feeding
(c) By allowing the cattle to graze in the fields
(d) By administering hormones

303 The Chief Commissioner of India holds office
(a) For Six years
(b) During the pleasure of the President
(c) For six years or till the age of 65 whichever is earlier
(d) For five years or till theage of 60 whichever is earlier

304 The day-to-day adminstration of a Union Territory in India is carried out by the
(a) President
(b) Governor
(c) Home Minister
(d) Lt. Governor

305 Which two States have a common High Court?
(a) Himachal Pradesh and Uttar Pradesh
(b) Haryana and Punjab
(c) Gujrat and Maharashtra
(d) Kerala and Tamil Nadu

306 How many members of the Anglo-Indian community may be nominated by the President in the Lok Sabha?
(a) Four
(b) Two
(c) Any number
(d) Only one

307 Who was the Chairman of the Constitution Assembly of India
(a) Dr. B. R. Ambedkar
(b) Dr. Rajendra Prassad
(c) Dr. B. N. Rau
(d) Pt. Jawahrlal Nehru

308 What is the duration of the membership of State Legislative Councils?
(a) 3 years
(b) 5 years
(c) 6 years
(d) 9 years

309 Vegetable oils are converted into solid fat (ghee) by
(a) Hydrolysis
(b) Addition of agar agar
(c) Oxidation using air and a catalyst
(d) Hydrogenation

310 An example of replenishable source of energy is
(a) Coal
(b) Petroleum

(c) Lignite
(d) Corticosteroid

311 A drug which helps in controlling fever is .
(a) Ibuprofen
(b) Penicillin
(c) Paracetamol
(d) Cortcosteroid

312 Identify the correct statement with respect to Biogas:
(a) Mixture of gases from volcanoes
(b) Gas produced from certain crude oil wells
(c) Gas produced by incomplete combustion of biomass
(d) Gas produced by fermentation of biomass

313 Aspartame is the name of a product used by the diabetic patients as a sweetening agent. It belongs to the class of
(a) Carbohydrates
(b) Peptides
(c) Polyhydric alcohols
(d) Alkaloids

314 If the price of Pepsi decreases relative to the price of Coke and 7-Up, the demand for
(a) Coke will decrease
(b) 7-up will decrease
(c) Cokd and 7-Up will increase
(d) Coke and 7-Up will decrease

315 The demand curve shows that the price and the quantity demanded are
(a) Directly related only
(b) Directly proportional and also directly related
(c) Inversely proportional and also inversely related
(d) Inversely related only

316 Which of the following is not a part of national income?
(a) Wages and Salaries
(b) Profits
(c) Rent
(d) Interest on national debt

317 Which of the following is not a part of tertiary sector
(a) Power and transportation

(b) Animal husbandry
(c) Cotton manufacturing
(d) Cultivation of crops

318 The largest share of India's national income originates in the
(a) Primary sector
(b) Secondary sector
(c) Tertiary sector
(d) None of the above

319 Fixed cost is known as
(a) Special cost
(b) Direct cost
(c) Prime cost
(d) Overhead cost

320 As output increases, average fixed cost
(a) Increases
(b) Falls
(c) Remains constant
(d) First increases then falls

321 The State which has developed wind energy is
(a) Gujrat
(b) Karnataka
(c) Kerala
(d) Andhra Pradesh

322 The continent through which the imaginary lines of tropic of Cancer, Tropic of Capricorn and Equator pass is
(a) Africa
(b) Australia
(c) Europe
(d) Asia

323 Which of the following countries has highest percentage of land under cultivation?
(a) U.S.A.
(b) India
(c) China
(d) Canada

324 Which of the following countries is known as the 'Land of Thunderbolt'?

(a) Belgium
(b) Nepal
(c) Bhutan
(d) Bolivia

325 The Melanesian Island Group lies in the
(a) Pecific Ocean
(b) Atlantic Ocean
(c) Indian Ocean
(d) Arctic Ocean

326 Which of the following planets is called evening star
(a) Mars
(b) Mercury
(c) Venus
(d) Jupiter

327 Great Barrier Reef of Austrlia is located parallel to the
(a) East coast
(b) West coast
(c) North Cost
(d) South coast

328 Which of the following is called 'Ring of Fire'?
(a) Circum Pacific Belt
(b) Mid Continental Belt
(c) Indian Ocean Belt
(d) Atlantic Ocean Belt

329 The scale that measure the intensity of earthquakes is called
(a) Vernier scale
(b) Richter scale
(c) Beaufort scale
(d) Diagonal Scale

330 The longest masonary dam has been constructed on the river
(a) Krishna
(b) Rihand
(c) Sutlej
(d) Mahanadi

331 The capital of Shivaji was
(a) Poona
(b) Raigadh

(c) Singadh
(d) Panhala

332 . Who was the court poet of Harsh
(a) Bhani
(b) Ravi Kirti
(c) Banabhatta
(d) Vishnu Sharma

333 Who among the following was famous for framing the education minute?
(a) Lord Elgin
(b) Lord Macaulay
(c) Sadler
(d) None of the above

334 Which among the following places was not an important centre of the Revolt of 1857?
(a) Agra
(b) Kanpur
(c) Jhansi
(d) Lucknow

335 Who among the following abolished the Dual System of Government of Bengal?
(a) Clive
(b) Lord Cornwalis
(c) Spencer
(d) Lord Warren Hestings

336 Swami Dayanand Saraswati established the first Arya Samaj in 1875 at
(a) Bombay
(b) Lahore
(c) Nagpur
(d) Ahmadnagar

337 Who among the following was the pioneer of social reform movements in the 19th century India?
(a) Aurobindo Ghosh
(b) Raja Rammohan Roy
(c) Devendra Nath Tagore
(d) Keshav Chandra Sen

338 The Second World War started in the year
(a) 1940
(b) 1939
(c) 1941
(d) 1942

339 Who among the following has been known as the'Frontier Gandhi'?
(a) Khan Abdul Gafar Khan
(b) Khan Saheb
(c) Chaudhary Shaukatullah
(d) Liyaquat Ali Khan

340 The Ryotwari System of Land Tenure refers to a situation where
(a) The Ryot is the owner of the land held by him/her and directly pays the revenue assessed on the land to the State
(b) The Ryot is an occupancy tenant of his/her land and pays the land revenus to the Zamindar
(c) The person cultivates the land leased in from a landlord and in return pays rent to the landlord
(d) The land is collectively owned and cultivated on a cooperative basis

341 Which of the following is the Japanese currancy?
(a) Taka
(b) Lira
(c) Mark
(d) Yen

342 Who invented the hydrogen bomb?
(a) J. Robert Oppenheimer
(b) Albert Einstein
(c) Samuel Cohen
(d) Edward Teller

343 Which district lies to the south of the district Tiruchirapalli?
(a) Villupuram
(b) Salem
(c) Vellore
(d) PuduKKottai

344 Who among the folowing is a distinguished Odissi dancer?
(a) Sonal Mansingh
(b) Sanyukta Panigrahi

(c) Sanyukta Narayan
(d) Hema Malini

345 Who is the Chairman of the National Human Rights Commission?
(a) Mr. Justice Ranganath Mishra
(b) Mr. Justice M. N. Venkatachalaiah
(c) Mr. Justice A. H. Ahmadi
(d) Mr. Justice J. S. Verma

346 Who among the following is a non-Indian who was conferred 'Bharat Ratna'?
(a) Mother Teressa
(b) Sheikh Mujibur Rehman
(c) Nelson Mandela
(d) Lord Mountbatten

347 'Liberty, Equality and Fretarnity' is the call associated with
(a) American Revolution
(b) French Revolution
(c) Chinese Revolution
(d) Russian Revolution

348 The instrument of music in which Ustad Amjad Ali Khan has distinguished himself is
(a) Sarod
(b) Violin
(c) Sitar
(d) Shehnai

349 Where is the lotus-shaped marble house of worship located?
(a) Mumbai
(b) Pune
(c) Delhi
(d) Agra

350 Who is the Solicitor-General of India?
(a) Ashok Desai
(b) N. Santosh Hegde
(c) Harish Salve
(d) S. B. Jaisinghani

351 Among the following tax revenues of the Union Government, which is the biggest source?
(a) Income Tax

(b) Corporation Tax
(c) Central Excise
(d) Customs Duty

352 What was the objective of the Command Area Development Programme?
(a) To ensure that land is given to the tillers
(b) To ensure better utilisation of irrigation potential
(c) To develope the area under the command Army
(d) Poverty alleviation in selected areas

353 Which country assisted India to established the Koodankulam Nuclear Power Station in Tamil Nadu?
(a) Russia
(b) Canada
(c) Germany
(d) France

354 The proposed Microsoft Software Development Centre in India is to be set up in
(a) Bangalore
(b) New Delhi
(c) Hyderabad
(d) Pune

355 Lion is conserved at
(a) Kaziranga Sanctuary
(b) Gir sanctuary
(c) Corbett National Park
(d) Masnas Sanctuary

356 The first World Cup in Cricket was held in
(a) 1975
(b) 1976
(c) 1983
(d) 1980

357 The only category in which either an Indian or a person of Indian origin has not got a Noble Prize is
(a) Medicine
(b) Chemistry
(c) Physics
(d) Literature

358 'Kuchipudi' is a dance style of
(a) Kerala
(b) Tamil Nadu
(c) Karnataka
(d) Andhra Pradesh

359 Which Indian cricketer holds the unique record of three consecutive centuries in his first three Tests?
(a) Saurav Ganguli
(b) Mohammad Azharuddin
(c) Surinder Amarnath
(d) Gundappa Vishwanath

360 The 2000 Olympic Games are scheduled to be held in
(a) Sydney
(b) Delhi
(c) Beijing
(d) Paris

361 Who among the following Governors of Punjab, responsible for the Jallianwalla Bagh massacre of 1919, was assassinated by Udham Singh in 1940?
(a) Sir Alfred Draper
(b) Sir Michael O'Dwyer
(c) Sir John O'Dwyer
(d) Sir John Lawrence

362 What was the name of the new English journal brought out by Gandhiji in 1933, replacing *Young India*?
(a) Shudra
(b) Harijan
(c) Al-Hilal
(d) Young Bharat

363 Which 13th Century Indian poet and disciple of Sufi Saint Hazrat Nizamuddin Aulia is buried next to his mentor in Delhi?
(a) Amir Khusro
(b) Salim Shah Chishti
(c) Moin-ud-din Chishti
(d) Kublai Khan

364 Which worldwide organisation owes its origin to a pamphlet called 'Un Souvenir de Solferino' written by Jean Henri Dunant in 1862?

(a) CARE
(b) Amnesty International
(c) International Red Cross
(d) Worldwide Vision

365 Which was the first general election in India to throw up a hung Parliament?
(a) 1889
(b) 1971
(c) 1977
(d) 1998

366 Men's team final of the NTPC Commomnwealth Table Tennis Championship, held during April 2001 in New Delhi was won by:
(a) England
(b) Singapore
(c) Nigeria
(d) India

367 Which one of the following liquid gas is used as a fuel for a cryogenic engine?
(a) Liquid Oxygen
(b) Liquid Hydrogen
(c) Liquid Nitrogen
(d) Liquid Chlorine

368 Sixteen Border Security Force personnel were killed in border clashes between the BSF and the Bangladesh Rifles during April 2001. These clashes occurred in:
(a) Dhubri, Assam
(b) Pyrdiwah, Meghalaya
(c) Dinga Amb, West Bengal
(d) Roamari, Bangladesh

369 Who among the following sports persons has not been chosen as one of the Persons of the year 2000 by the Limca Book of Records?
(a) IWM Vijaylakshmi
(b) Boxer N. Dingko Singh
(c) Footballer Baichung Bhutia
(d) Footballer I. M. Vijayan

370 Which one of the following is not the highlight of the RBI's

Monetary and Credit Policy for the first half (April-Oct.) of the fiscal 2001-02?

(a) Interest rate on export credit reduced by 1 to 1.5 percent
(b) CRR made more flexible, Interest on CRR balance decreased
(c) RBI to divest its ownership in financial institutions
(d) Senior citizens to get higher interest on deposits

371 Who among the following is a Bharatnatyam dancer?

(a) Kaushalya Reddy
(b) Navtej Singh Johar
(c) Sunil Mehra
(d) Rajeev Lochan

372 Which of the following is not one of the three basic instruments carried by NASA's Mars Mission-*2001* : A Space Odyssey?

(a) MARIE
(b) GRS
(c) THEMIS
(d) DANICS

373 Who among the following is himself a sitarist, Sanskrit Award winner and son of the sitarist Pandit Kartik Kumar of Senia Gharana?

(a) Niladri Kumar
(b) Hemadri Kumar
(c) Gaurav Mazumdar
(d) Manohar Dasgupta

374 Osteoporosis is a disease that effects:

(a) Heart
(b) Lungs
(c) Bones
(d) Kidneys

375 Who among the following is the part owner of Mir Corp, which is selling a multi-million dollar dream for 20 million dollar and has made Dennis Tito, the first space tourist to International Space Station?

(a) Chiranjeev Kathuria
(b) Vikram Kathuria
(c) Vikram Raina

(d) Chiranjeev Kumar

376 Who among the following is the Chairman of the Hurriyat Party?
(a) Syed Mir Qasim
(b) Bashir Ahmed Bhat
(c) Syed Ali Geelani
(d) Abdul Ghani Bhat

377 2001 Pulitzer prize for public service and feature writing is won by which of the following papers?
(a) Rutland Herald
(b) Miami Herald
(c) Chicago Tribune
(d) The Oregonian

378 Who among the following has been appointed as the Acting Director of the Central Bureau of Investigation?
(a) K. Chakravarthy
(b) P. C. Sharma
(c) R. K. Raghavan
(d) H. K. Dora

379 Who among the following is the author of the book *Notes on the Great Indian Circus*?
(a) Mira Seth
(b) Harsh Mander
(c) Khushwant Singh
(d) Ravi Chaturvedi

380 According to the 13th Rich list of *The Sunday Times,* who among the following is the wealthiest person on the planet?
(a) Larry Ellison (Oracle)
(b) Bill Gates (Microsoft)
(c) King Fahd (Saudi Arabia)
(d) S. Robson Walton (Wal-Mart)

381 Teledensity at the end of 1999-2000 in India approximately stands at:
(a) 3.54%
(b) 3.15%
(c) 2.86%
(d) 2.15%

382 Who among the following is the new President of the Confederation of Indian Industry?
(a) Ashok Soota
(b) Sanjeev Goenka
(c) D. K. Ghoshal
(d) Tarun Das

383 Which of the following is not a mascot for the 2002 Football World Cup?
(a) Ato
(b) Nik
(c) Kaz
(d) Mik

384 'Darshak', which was the news during April 2001, is a/an
(a) Indigenously-built hydrographic survey ship commissioned into the Indian Navy
(b) Indigenously-built submarine commissioned into the Indian Navy
(c) Indigenously-built missile frigate commissioned into the Indian Navy
(d) None of these

385 Women's team event of the World Table Tennis Championship held at Osaka during April 2001 was won by:
(a) North Korea
(b) South Korea
(c) Japan
(d) China

386 According to the recent World Development Report, India's economy in Purchasing Power Parity, measured in 1999 US prices, has been ranked:
(a) Fourth
(b) Fifth
(c) Sixth
(d) Seventh

387 Who among the following is not a coach at the North Zone Cricket Academy?
(a) Yash Pal Sharma
(b) Chetan Sharma

(c) Surinder Sharma
(d) Rajinder Amarnath

388 Majuli the world's largest riverine island, is surrounded by waters of the river:
(a) Amazon
(b) Ganga
(c) Brahmaputra
(d) Nile

389 Who among the following is the recepient of Saraswati Samman for the Year 2000 for his novel *Amruta Phala?*
(a) Dr. Indira Parthasarathy
(b) Manoj Das
(c) Sri Ramakant Rath
(d) Subir Das

390 'Operation Purna Vijay' is associated with:
(a) Indian Army's military exercise conducted in May 2001 in Thar desert
(b) Indian Navy's military exercise in May 2001 in Bay of Bengal
(c) BSF's attack on Bangladesh border in Assam
(d) None of these

391 Which one of the following Governors-General is credited with the extermination of the Pindaris?
(a) Lord Hastings
(b) Lord Hardings
(c) Lord Clive
(d) Lord Curzon

392 The founder of the Slave Dynasty in India was?
(a) Qutub-ud-din Aibak
(b) Iltutmish
(c) Aram Shah
(d) Kaiquabad

393 In military technology, 'zero hour' means:
(a) Midnight
(b) Expected time of withdrawl
(c) Expected time of attack
(d) Expected time of surrender

394 City of Seven Hills is the same as the:
(a) City of Eternal Springs
(b) Eternal City
(c) Forbidden City
(d) City of Palaces

395 Which one of the following is matched correctly?
(a) Jantar Mantar - Udaipur
(b) Marble Rocks - Jabalpur
(c) Victoria Memorial - Mumbai
(d) Pichola Lake - Srinagar

396 Tha Gandhi Peace Award for 1998 has gone to:
(a) Rama Krishna Mission
(b) Buddha Peace Foundation
(c) Missionaries of Charity
(d) Dalai Lama

397 Which event in cricket has been recently started on an experimental basis?
(a) Pepsi Independence Cup
(b) Asian Cup of One-day Matches
(c) Asian Cup of Test Matches
(d) Ashes

398 Who got the 1998 Jnanpith Award?
(a) V. R. Ananth Murthy
(b) M. T. Vasudevan Nair
(c) Ali Sardar Jafri
(d) Girish Karnad

399 Which one of the following amendments to the Indian Constitution incorporated the Fundamental Duties of Citizens?
(a) 41st
(b) 42nd
(c) 43rd
(d) 44th

400 Which one of the following is *not* an archipelago?
(a) Lakshadweep
(b) Sri Lanka
(c) Maldives
(d) Andaman & Nicobar

401 During whose Prime Ministership of Britain did India gain freedom?
(a) Chamberlain
(b) Churchill
(c) Attlee
(d) MacDonald

402 Which of the following parts/tissues of the body can be safely transplanted in the body of another person without any problem of rejection or reaction?
(a) Kidney
(b) Heart
(c) Skin
(d) Cornea

403 Of the following States which one depends for its tea requirements entirely on other states?
(a) Andhra Pradesh
(b) Karnataka
(c) Kerala
(d) Tamil Nadu

404 Who among the following was the Founder of the Atomic Theory?
(a) Benjamin Franklin
(b) Madame Curie
(c) Albert Einstein
(d) John Dalton

405 Which one of the following is not correctly matched?
(a) Ravi Shankar - Sitarist
(b) M. F. Hussain - Tabla Player
(c) R. K. Narayan - Novelist
(d) Kaifi Azmi - Poet

406 Name the author of *Ramayan Darshnam.*
(a) G. Shankar Kurup
(b) V. Satyanarayan
(c) K. V. Puttapa
(d) T. S. Pillai

407 What is the percentage of carbohydrates in the normal daily food calorie requirement of an adult?
(a) About 7%
(b) About 35%

(c) About 48%
(d) About 59%

408 Which one of the classical dance forms originated in Andhra Pradesh?
(a) Bharat Natyam
(b) Kathakali
(c) Kuchipudi
(d) Oddissy

409 Which one of the following cities is an important centre of aircraft industry in India?
(a) Bangalore
(b) Chennai
(c) Hyderabad
(d) Nagpur

410 In which State is the People's War Group operative?
(a) J & K
(b) Orissa
(c) Andhra Pradesh
(d) Manipur

411 Who was the first woman President of the United Nations Organisation?
(a) Vijaylaxmi Pandit
(b) Rajkumari Amrit Kaur
(c) S. Bandarnaike
(d) Sarojini Naidu

412 With which aspect of commerce are the Bull and Bears associated?
(a) Foreign Trade
(b) Stock Market
(c) Internal Trade
(d) Banking

413 Which three of the following were the Dravida Kingdoms in India?
(a) Saka, Gandhar, Magadha
(b) Avanti, Telang, Mahakossala
(c) Satvahana, Kalinga, Rashtrakuta
(d) Chola, Pandya, Chera

414 Tropical forests in Silent Valley lie in the State of:
(a) Goa

(b) Karnataka
(c) Kerala
(d) Tamil Nadu

415 Shanghai is situated on the river:
(a) Hwang Ho
(b) Yangtze Kiang
(c) Min Chiang
(d) Hsiang

416 Madumalai Sanctuary is located in:
(a) Andhra Pradesh
(b) Karnataka
(c) Kerala
(d) Tamil Nadu

417 The Battle of Wandiwash was fought between the English and:
(a) The French
(b) The Portuguese
(c) The Marathas
(d) The Sultan

418 Who discovered the neutron?
(a) John Bardeen
(b) William Brag
(c) Henry Cavendish
(d) James Chadwick

419 With which event in 1991 brought about a great change in the world political scene?
(a) Unification of the two Germanys
(b) Disintegration of USSR
(c) The Gulf War
(d) Stoppage of Military aid to Pakistan by USA

420 Impure blood is received in the heart in the:
(a) Right auricle
(b) Left auricle
(c) Right ventricle
(d) Left ventricle

421 Which one of the following is not correctly matched:
(a) Colossium - Rome
(b) Kremlin - Moscow

(c) Wall Street - New York
(d) White Hall - Washington

422 In the history of the world, which one of the following revolutions has been the latest?
(a) Red Revolution in China
(b) French Revolution
(c) Glorious Revolution in England
(d) Russian Revolution

423 The headquarters of UNESCO is at:
(a) The Hague
(b) New York
(c) Paris
(d) Washington

424 Which one of the following is not correctly matched?
(a) Bhangra - Punjab
(b) Bihu - Manipur
(c) Garba - Gujarat
(d) Tamasha - Maharashtra

425 Who wrote *The Hindu view of Life*?
(a) S. Radhakrishnan
(b) Sri Aurobindo
(c) Rabindra Nath Tagore
(d) Swami Vivekananda

426 Which new championship was introduced in the last Commonwealth Games held in Malaysia?
(a) Cricket
(b) Football
(c) Hockey
(d) Tennis

427 To which of the following political parties did the 12th Lok Sabha Speaker belong
(a) BJP
(b) TMC
(c) INLD
(d) TDP

428 Which one of the following unfortunate events is an illustration of class-conflict?

(a) Burning to death of a missionary and his two sons in Orissa
(b) Gunning down of Dalits in Bihar
(c) Pulling down of churches in Gujarat
(d) Crushing to death of a college girl by some youths in Madhya Pradesh

429 Which one of the following is an anti-tank missile?
(a) Agni
(b) Nag
(c) Prithvi
(d) Trishul

430 All the following hotels are owned by ITDC except
(a) Ashoka
(b) Qutub
(c) Maurya
(d) Samrat

431 Stainless steel is an alloy whereas air is a
(a) Gas
(b) Mixture
(c) Compound
(d) Solution

432 After every general elections which House (s) of the Parliament is (are) reconstituted?
(a) Rajya Sabha
(b) Lok Sabha
(c) Both Houses of Parliament
(d) None because both the Houses have some nominees

433 Sunderlal Bahuguna has acquired fame on account of his contribution to the preservation of:
(a) Tigers
(b) Forests
(c) Marine Life
(d) Rare species of birds

434 The Chief Guest at the 1999 Republic day Parade was the
(a) President of South Africa
(b) King of Nepal
(c) President of Sri Lanka
(d) President of France

435 The 1999 National Games of India were held at:

(a) Bangalore (b) Kolkata
(c) Guwahati (d) Imphal

436 What is 'Patriot'

(a) It is a surface-to-air anti-aircraft missile
(b) It is a nuclear warhead
(c) It is an anti-missile system
(d) It is a powerful bomber

437 List I below gives names of four important places and List II their locations. Match these and say which one of the four alternatives given under the lists give a correct matching.

List I	List II
(a) Birla Planetarium	(A) Guwahati
(b) Elephanta Caves	(B) Mumbai
(c) Hazrat Bal	(C) Kolkata
(d) Kamakhya Temple	(D) Srinagar

	A	B	C	D
(i)	c	b	d	a
(ii)	b	a	c	d
(iii)	a	d	b	c
(iv)	a	b	c	d

438 Name the author of *Worshipping False Gods* ?

(a) Khushwant Singh
(b) Arundhati Roy
(c) Salman Rushdie
(d) Arun Shourie

439 Considering the time of the sunrise from the earlist to the latest, which four cities are in the correct order?

(a) Guwahati - Patna - Burdwan - Nagpur
(b) Chennai - Bhubaneshwar - Hyderabad - Vishakhapatnam
(c) Tezpur - Kolkata - Raipur - Kota
(d) Panaji - Bangalore - Pondicherry - Calicut

440 Asteroids revolve round the Sun between

(a) Mars and Jupiter
(b) Earth and Mars
(c) Saturn and Uranus
(d) Uranus and Neptune

441 Who among the foreign travellers was the first to visit India?
(a) Hieun Tsang
(b) Ibn-Batutah
(c) Marco Polo
(d) Fa Hien

442 Most of the Ajanta paintings were completed during the rule of the:
(a) Vardhanas
(b) Sakas
(c) Satvahanas
(d) Guptas

443 Malik Kafur was a general of:
(a) Sikander Lodhi
(b) Qutub-ud-din-Aibak
(c) Ala-ud-din-Khilji
(d) Humayun

444 Buddhism in Nepal was introduced in the reign of:
(a) Samudragupta
(b) Ashoka
(c) Chandragupta
(d) Harsha

445 Shanti Swarup Bhatnagar is known for his:
(a) Fine literary works in Urdu and English
(b) Remarkable scientific achievements
(c) Leading a movement for social reforms
(d) Great concern for the uplift of the poor

446 Asteroids revolve round the Sun between Provincial autonomy was provided in the Government of India Act of:
(a) 1909
(b) 1935
(c) 1919
(d) None of these

447 The Government of India Act of 1935 was characterised as a 'new charter of slavery' by:
(a) Jawaharlal Nehru
(b) Sardar Patel
(c) M. K. Gandhi

(d) Abul Kalam Azad

448 Which layer of atmosphere provides ideal conditions for flying aeroplane
(a) Troposphere
(b) Stratosphere
(c) Ionosphere
(d) Exosphere

449 Who among the following is known as Father of the Indian Constitution?
(a) Dr. Rajendra Prasad
(b) Dr. B. R. Ambedkar
(c) Dr. S. Radhakrishnan
(d) M. K. Gandhi

450 Which of the following pairs is not correctly matched?
(a) Panna - Diamond
(b) Neyveli - Lignite
(c) Mysore - Marble
(d) Sambhar - Salt

451 The earthquake waves which have transverse movements are known as:
(a) Primary waves
(b) Secondary waves
(c) Surface waves
(d) None of the above

452 The first man to reach the South Pole on December 14, 1911 was:
(a) Commander Robert, E. Peary of U. S. Navy
(b) Racald Amundsen from Norway
(c) The Navigator Ferdinand Magellan
(d) Sir Francis Drake of England

453 Which one of the following is *not* the vegetation in Selva forests?
(a) Epiphytes
(b) Xerophytes
(c) Lianas
(d) Hydrophytes

454 Where does the primitive community of Bushman live?
(a) Sahara desert
(b) Thar desert

(c) Kalahari desert
(d) Attacama desert

455 Which region of India receives rainfall due to western disturbances in Winter?
(a) Western region
(b) Central Region
(c) Eastern Region
(d) North-western region

456 Which of the following countries had the highest foreign exchange reserves at the end of December 1999
(a) China
(b) Japan
(c) Taiwan
(d) Singapore

457 The large scale monocrop agriculture resembling factory production is:
(a) Mixed farming
(b) Plantation agriculture
(c) Shifting agriculture
(d) Commercial agriculture

458 Two goods are substitutes of each other if:
(a) Both are manufactured by the same factory
(b) One can be used in place of other
(c) Both of them are consumed simultaneously
(d) The price of one is similar to the other

459 The term 'Green Revolution' stands for:
(a) Large scale afforestation
(b) Large scale reduction in soil erosion
(c) Rapid growth in the output of green vegetables
(d) Rapid increase in agricultural productivity

460 The theory that 'Interest is the reward for parting with liquidity for a specific period' is propounded by:
(a) Prof. Joseph Schumpeter
(b) Lord Keynes
(c) Prof. F. H. Knight
(d) Alfred Marshall

461 Which bank in India first introduced the Credit Card System.
(a) Andhra Bank
(b) Central Bank
(c) Canara Bank
(d) State Bank of India

462 The maximum amount of revenue collected by Government of India is from:
(a) Customs duties
(b) Income and expenditure taxes
(c) Corporation Tax
(d) Excise duties

463 The act or process by which an alien is allowed to enjoy the privileges of a citizen of a country and ceases to be an alien is:
(a) Neutralisation
(b) Nationalisation
(c) Naturalisation
(d) Repatriation

464 In India a bank is obliged to maintain a Statute Liquidity ratio which is the ratio of its:
(a) Cash holdings to its deposit liabilities
(b) Cash holdings to its total liabilities
(c) Specified assets to its deposit liabilities
(d) Specified assets to its total liabilities

465 A Proclamation of Emergency (under Article 356) ceases to operate (unless approved and extended by Parliament) at the end of:
(a) One month
(b) Two months
(c) Three months
(d) Six months

466 The Association of South East Asian Nations (ASEAN) has its headquarters at:
(a) Manila
(b) Jakarta
(c) Kualalampur
(d) Bangkok

467 Which of the following subjects of the Concurrent List was

originally placed in the State List?
(a) Electricity
(b) Newspapers
(c) Education
(d) Marriage and divorce

468 Which is wrongly paired?

Schedule of the Constitution	*Subject Matter*
(a) First Schedule	- Allocation of seats in Council of States
(b) Seventh Schedule	- Division of Powers between Union and States
(c) Eighth Schedule	- Official Languages
(d) Tenth Schedule	- Disqualification on grounds of defection

469 A bill becomes a law when:
(a) Both Houses of Parliament approve it by requisite majority
(b) The Council of Ministers approves it
(c) The President gives his assent
(d) The Supreme Court upholds its constitutional validity

470 The genetic information is stored in:
(a) DNA
(b) RNA
(c) Ribosome
(d) Endoplasmic reticulum

471 Certain Bacteria living in human digestive system are beneficial because they synthesize vitamin
(a) D
(b) B-Complex
(c) K
(d) A

472 Who examines the report of the Controller and Auditor-General of India after it is laid before Parliament?
(a) Lok Sabha Speaker
(b) Estimates Committee
(c) Public Accounts Committee
(d) None of the above

473 The inorganic natural resource of the earth is:
(a) Mineral fuels
(b) Wood
(c) Coal
(d) Microbes

474 Teflon used for coating non-stick kitchenware is the product of chance discovery by the scientist
(a) Roy J. Pulunkett
(b) Johannes George Bednorz
(c) Karl Alexander Muller
(d) William Henry Perkin

475 A dispersion of tiny droplets of one liquid in another is known as:
(a) Emulsion
(b) Sol
(c) Gel
(d) Lyophilic colloid

476 Change in colour of stars arises due to:
(a) Variation in their distance from the earth
(b) Variation in their surface temperature
(c) Fluctuations in their composition and size
(d) Irregular absorption or scattering in earth's atmosphere

477 The catalyst used during the cracking of petroleum is:
(a) A mixture of alumina and silica
(b) Zinc oxide
(c) Activated charcoal
(d) Finely divided nickel

478 Who among the following players has taken more than 500 wickets in Test Cricket?
(a) Kapil Dev
(b) Wasim Akram
(c) Courtney Walsh
(d) Curtly Ambrose

479 Kwashiorkor is a disease in which victims, particularly growing children, become lethargic, get oedema and fail to grow normally. This disease occurs due to the deficiency in the diet of:
(a) Fats

(b) Minerals
(c) Proteins
(d) Vitamins

480 Which of the following has high iron content?
(a) Cheese
(b) Egg
(c) Green Vegetables
(d) Milk

481 Who among the following has not been a Prime Minister of Pakistan?
(a) Liaqat Ali Khan
(b) Ayub Khan
(c) Benazir Bhutto
(d) Nawaz Sharief

482 Who among the following was recently crowned Miss Universe 2001?
(a) Miss Greece
(b) Miss U.S.A.
(c) Miss Puerto Rico
(d) Miss India

483 Harare is the capital of:
(a) Congo
(b) Zanzibar
(c) Zambia
(d) Zimbabwe

484 Soli J. Sorabjee is the:
(a) Law Secretary, Government of India
(b) Solicitor-General of India
(c) Attorney-General of India
(d) Chairman, Law Commission

485 How many One-Day Internationals have been played in Sharjah (U.A.E.) till May 2001?
(a) 166
(b) 170
(c) 174
(d) 178

486 Which of the following States is ruled by a Congress Government?
(a) West Bengal
(b) Orissa
(c) Karnataka
(d) Jammu and Kashmir

487 Granivorous animals are those that live on:
(a) Grams and grains of different type
(b) Grass
(c) Human flesh
(d) Animal flesh

488 The Oscar Award for the Best Film for 2001 has been given to:
(a) Crouching Tiger
(b) American Beauty
(c) Gladiator
(d) Shakespeare in Love

489 The 1999 Dadasaheb Phalke Award has been given to:
(a) B. R. Chopra
(b) Hrishikesh Mukherjee
(c) Kavi Pradeep
(d) Shivaji Ganesan

490 Who was the Chief Guest at the Republic Day Parade, 2001?
(a) Bill Clinton
(b) Abdelaziz Bouteflika
(c) Tony Blair
(d) Aerial Sharon

491 Kalpana Chawla became world famous because:
(a) She was crowned the Miss Universe title
(b) She successfully completed the voyage in a US spacecraft
(c) She was the first Indian woman Senator in USA
(d) Her novel in English won the Pulitzer Prize

492 The name 'Prasar Bharati' refers to:
(a) A popular television entertainment programme
(b) A Hindi journal on entertainment media
(c) An autonomous Board for Doordarshan and Akashvani
(d) External Radio Programme for expatriate Indians

493 *Nag* is the name of the indigenously developed

(a) Medium Range Missile
(b) Anti-tank Missile
(c) Torpedo
(d) Submarine

494 The name of the first Indian-made Super Computer is:
(a) Param 10000
(b) Sankhyiki 1998
(c) Arya Bhatta
(d) Mahan Ganit

495 The author of the book *The God of Small Things* is:
(a) Arundhati Roy
(b) Mahasweta Devi
(c) Shobha De
(d) Amita Malik

496 Tony Blair, The Prime Minister of the United kingdom, belongs to the:
(a) Conservative Party
(b) Liberal Party
(c) Labour Party
(d) Social Democratic Party

497 The African country Burkina Faso was earlier known as:
(a) Northern Rhodesia
(b) Orange Free State
(c) Upper Volta
(d) Gold Coast

498 The Official Languages of the United Nations Organisation are:
(a) English, French, Russian, Chinese and German
(b) English, French, Chinese, Russian and Spanish
(c) German, Chinese, Hindi, English and French
(d) English, French, Chinese, Spanish, and Japanese

499 Macedonia, from which 'Alexander the Great' came, was till recently part of which country?
(a) Greece
(b) Italy
(c) Albania
(d) Yugoslavia

500 The purpose of choke in tube light is:
(a) To decrease the current
(b) To increase the current
(c) To decrease the voltage momentarily
(d) To increase the voltage momentarily

501 The three primary colours used in colour television are:
(a) Red, Yellow, Violet
(b) Yellow, Green, Violet
(c) Red, Green, Blue
(d) Yellow, Blue, Violet

502 When an electric fan moves slow, it consumes
(a) More energy than that when it moves fast
(b) Less energy than that when it moves fast
(c) The same amount of energy as it will do when it moves fast
(d) None of the above

503 The tape of a tape-recorder is coated with
(a) Copper Sulphate
(b) Ferromagnetic powder
(c) Silica
(d) Zinc Sulphide

504 LPG consists mainly of:
(a) Methane, Etane and Hexane
(b) Ethane, Hexane and Nonane
(c) Methane, Butane and Propane
(d) Ethane, Nonane and Hexane

505 The carbon used in printer's ink is:
(a) Charcoal
(b) Carbon Black
(c) Gas Carbon
(d) Coke

506 AIDS is confirmed by:
(a) HIV^+
(b) HIV^-
(c) Blood grouping
(d) Blood cell counting

507 The largest gland in human body is:
(a) Salivary

(b) Pituitary
(c) Pancreas
(d) Liver

508 Glaucoma is a disease of the:
(a) Skin
(b) Lungs
(c) Liver
(d) Eyes

509 Which of the following cannot be controlled by vaccination?
(a) Small-pox
(b) Diabetes
(c) Whooping Cough
(d) Polio

510 Bhagat Singh was hanged for which of the following reasons?
(a) For participating in the Vande Mataram Movement
(b) For participating in the Jallianwala Bagh incident
(c) For the participation in Kolkata conspiracy case
(d) For killing General Saunders

511 National Flag was designed by:
(a) Mahatma Gandhi
(b) Subhash Chandra Bose
(c) Jawaharlal Nehru
(d) Pingali Venkayya

512 Hiuen-Tsang visited India during the reign of:
(a) Harsh Vardhana
(b) Skanda Gupta
(c) Chandragupta Maurya
(d) Ashoka

513 The crop which grows well in sandy soils is:
(a) Sandal wood
(b) Bamboo
(c) Teak
(d) Coconut

514 Epicentre is:
(a) Focus of earthquake
(b) Location of earthquake
(c) Area coverage of earthquake

(d) Core of earthquake

515 Which city is known as the Pearl of the Orient?
(a) Yangoon
(b) Singapore
(c) Bangkok
(d) Tokyo

Answers

1	(a)	2	(b)	3	(a)	4	(a)	5	(c)
6	(b)	7	(c)	8	(a)	9	(c)	10	(c)
11	(b)	12	(c)	13	(a)	14	(d)	15	(b)
16	(a)	17	(c)	18	(b)	19	(a)	20	(a)
21	(a)	22	(c)	23	(b)	24	(c)	25	(c)
26	(a)	27	(b)	28	(a)	29	(b)	30	(a)
31	(b)	32	(d)	33	(d)	34	(c)	35	(b)
36	(c)	37	(a)	38	(a)	39	(a)	40	(c)
41	(b)	42	(a)	43	(b)	44	(b)	45	(a)
46	(c)	47	(b)	48	(a)	49	(a)	50	(a)
51	(c)	52	(b)	53	(b)	54	(a)	55	(d)
56	(b)	57	(a)	58	(d)	59	(c)	60	(a)
61	(b)	62	(c)	63	(c)	64	(b)	65	(b)
66	(d)	67	(c)	68	(b)	69	(a)	70	(b)
71	(a)	72	(b)	73	(c)	74	(d)	75	(a)
76	(b)	77	(a)	78	(d)	79	(c)	80	(b)
81	(c)	82	(c)	83	(b)	84	(c)	85	(b)
86	(c)	87	(a)	88	(b)	89	(c)	90	(b)
91	(b)	92	(d)	93	(a)	94	(a)	95	(c)
96	(d)	97	(b)	98	(c)	99	(b)	100	(a)
101	(b)	102	(c)	103	(d)	104	(d)	105	(b)
106	(a)	107	(b)	108	(c)	109	(c)	110	(b)
111	(b)	112	(c)	113	(c)	114	(c)	115	(d)
116	(d)	117	(b)	118	(a)	119	(b)	120	(b)

121	(b)	122	(c)	123	(b)	124	(b)	125	(a)
126	(c)	127	(a)	128	(d)	129	(d)	130	(b)
131	(c)	132	(d)	133	(c)	134	(c)	135	(b)
136	(b)	137	(a)	138	(c)	139	(c)	140	(d)
141	(c)	142	(b)	143	(c)	144	(d)	145	(a)
146	(c)	147	(b)	148	(d)	149	(a)	150	(a)
151	(a)	152	(a)	153	(b)	154	(b)	155	(d)
156	(d)	157	(a)	158	(b)	159	(b)	160	(b)
161	(b)	162	(d)	163	(c)	164	(a)	165	(c)
166	(b)	167	(a)	168	(b)	169	(a)	170	(d)
171	(a)	172	(a)	173	(c)	174	(a)	175	(a)
176	(c)	177	(a)	178	(b)	179	(c)	180	(c)
181	(d)	182	(c)	183	(b)	184	(a)	185	(d)
186	(b)	187	(c)	188	(b)	189	(b)	190	(b)
191	(a)	192	(b)	193	(a)	194	(b)	195	(c)
196	(d)	197	(a)	198	(a)	199	(a)	200	(d)
201	(b)	202	(b)	203	(a)	204	(c)	205	(b)
206	(d)	207	(c)	208	(c)	209	(b)	210	(a)
211	(c)	212	(a)	213	(a)	214	(b)	215	(a)
216	(b)	217	(a)	218	(c)	219	(c)	220	(d)
221	(c)	222	(a)	223	(c)	224	(b)	225	(c)
226	(b)	227	(c)	228	(a)	229	(b)	230	(b)
231	(c)	232	(a)	233	(c)	234	(c)	235	(c)
236	(c)	237	(b)	238	(d)	239	(d)	240	(c)
241	(d)	242	(a)	243	(a)	244	(d)	245	(b)
246	(c)	247	(a)	248	(b)	249	(a)	250	(a)
251	(c)	252	(a)	253	(b)	254	(b)	255	(c)
256	(c)	257	(c)	258	(a)	259	(d)	260	(c)
261	(a)	262	(c)	263	(a)	264	(c)	265	(b)
266	(d)	267	(a)	268	(a)	269	(b)	270	(c)

271	(b)	272	(b)	273	(a)	274	(b)	275	(d)
276	(a)	277	(a)	278	(c)	279	(a)	280	(d)
281	(a)	282	(c)	283	(c)	284	(c)	285	(c)
286	(d)	287	(a)	288	(a)	289	(b)	290	(a)
291	(d)	292	(b)	293	(a)	294	(c)	295	(a)
296	(b)	297	(d)	298	(a)	299	(d)	300	(b)
301	(c)	302	(b)	303	(c)	304	(a)	305	(a)
306	(b)	307	(c)	308	(c)	309	(c)	310	(a)
311	(b)	312	(c)	313	(d)	314	(a)	315	(a)
316	(a)	317	(b)	318	(c)	319	(d)	320	(d)
321	(b)	322	(a)	323	(d)	324	(a)	325	(a)
326	(a)	327	(a)	328	(d)	329	(c)	330	(a)
331	(b)	332	(b)	333	(b)	334	(b)	335	(c)
336	(a)	337	(a)	338	(c)	339	(a)	340	(b)
341	(b)	342	(c)	343	(c)	344	(b)	345	(d)
346	(c)	347	(b)	348	(a)	349	(a)	350	(b)
351	(a)	352	(a)	353	(d)	354	(b)	355	(b)
356	(a)	357	(c)	358	(a)	359	(a)	360	(c)
361	(b)	362	(b)	363	(a)	364	(c)	365	(a)
366	(c)	367	(b)	368	(a)	369	(c)	370	(b)
371	(b)	372	(d)	373	(a)	374	(c)	375	(a)
376	(d)	377	(d)	378	(b)	379	(c)	380	(d)
381	(c)	382	(b)	383	(d)	384	(a)	385	(d)
386	(a)	387	(c)	388	(c)	389	(b)	390	(a)
391	(a)	392	(a)	393	(c)	394	(b)	395	(b)
396	(a)	397	(c)	398	(d)	399	(b)	400	(b)
401	(c)	402	(d)	403	(a)	404	(d)	405	(b)
406	(3)	407	(d)	408	(c)	409	(a)	410	(c)
411	(a)	412	(b)	413	(d)	414	(c)	415	(b)
416	(d)	417	(a)	418	(d)	419	(b)	420	(a)

421	(a)	422	(a)	423	(c)	424	(b)	425	(a)
426	(d)	427	(b)	428	(b)	429	(b)	430	(c)
431	(b)	432	(a)	433	(b)	434	(b)	435	(d)
436	(a)	437	(a)	438	(d)	439	(c)	440	(a)
441	(d)	442	(d)	443	(c)	444	(b)	445	(b)
446	(b)	447	(a)	448	(a	449	(b)	450	(c)
451	(b)	452	(b)	453	(b)	454	(c)	455	(c)
456	(b	457	(d)	458	(b)	459	(d)	460	(b)
461	(c)	462	(d)	463	(c)	464	(c)	465	(b)
466	(a)	467	(a)	468	(d)	469	(c)	470	(b)
471	(b)	472	(a)	473	(b)	474	(b)	475	(d)
476	(d)	477	(a)	478	(c)	479	(c)	480	(c)
481	(b)	482	(c)	483	(d)	484	(c)	485	(c)
486	(c)	487	(a)	488	(c)	489	(b)	490	(b)
491	(b)	492	(c)	493	(b)	494	(a)	495	(a)
496	(a)	497	(a)	498	(d)	499	(c)	500	(c)
501	(c)	502	(a)	503	(d)	504	(c)	505	(b)
506	(a)	507	(b)	508	(d)	509	(a)	510	(d)
511	(d)	512	(a)	513	(d)	514	(d)	515	(c)

MISCELLANEOUS & GENERAL KNOWLEDGE

1 The millennium Film Star Amitabh Bachchan unveiled his life-like figure in Madame Tussaud's wax Museum in December 2000. This museum is located in which of the following cities?
(a) Moscow
(b) New York
(c) London
(d) Paris

2 Seven sacred rivers of India are collectively known as
(a) Sapta Sindhu
(b) Sapta Teerth
(c) Sapta Mukhi
(d) Sapta Vahini

3 In which daily newspaper started by her in August 1914, Annie Besant popularised the slogan 'Home Rule'?
(a) India
(b) New India
(c) Herald
(d) Sarawak

4 Which region in India was once known as Avantika?
(a) Bundelkhand
(b) Avadh
(c) Malwa
(d) Mewar

5 Who among the following built the fortification in Aravallies sometimes also called the great wall of India?
(a) Rana Sanga
(b) Man Singh
(c) Rana Pratap
(d) Rana Kumbha

6 International Corporation for Assigned Names and Numbers (ICANN) has approved new domain names suffixes ending the monopoly of dotcoms (.coms) over domain names. Which of the following sets does not have an approved name?
(a) .aero, .name, .coop

(b) .pro, .info, .biz
(c) .museum, .name, .coop
(d) .games, .info, .pro

7 Birla Institute of Technology & Sciences, Pilani (Rajasthan), is setting up an Engineering Education Centre in Dubai in collaboration with which one of Dubai?
(a) Al Ghurair
(b) Al Questech
(c) Al-Hajar
(d) Al Heidel

8 ICICI Ltd., country's leading financial services provider, has appointed whom among the following as its brand ambassador for two years?
(a) Sachin Tendulkar
(b) Amitabh Bachchan
(c) Sunil Gavaskar
(d) Shahrukh Khan

9 S P S Rathor was in the news during November 2000 in view of a CBI chargesheet filed against him for the alleged molestation of a girl. He is the Director-General of Police of which of following States?
(a) Rajsthan
(b) Madhya Pradesh
(c) Punjab
(d) Haryana

10 Who among the following is the recipient of 1999 Indira Gandhi Prize for Peace, Disarmament and Development?
(a) Prof. M. S. Swaminathan
(b) Mr. Krishan Kant
(c) Mr. K. C. Pant
(d) Mr. A. Balsubramaniam

11 Which among the following countries is the current Chairman of SAARC?
(a) India
(b) Sri Lanka
(c) Pakistan
(d) Bangladesh

12 A Pakistani Court has issued a summon for former England Captain Michael Atherton in a $200,000 defamation suit filed by a Pakistani journalist. Who among the following is this journalist?

(a) Abdur Razzak
(b) Saqlain Ahmed
(c) Asgher Ali
(d) Asghar Ahmed

13 Who among the following is the current president of Shiromani Gurudwara Prabandhak Committee?

(a) Jagdev Singh Talwandi
(b) Balbir Singh Pannu
(c) Hardalbir Singh Shah
(d) Prakash Singh Badal

14 Who among the following became the first Speaker of the Jharkhand Assembly?

(a) Teklal Mahto
(b) Niel Tirkey
(c) Girinath Singh
(d) Inder Singh Namdhari

15 Third World Chess Championship was held during December 2000 in

(a) New Delhi
(b) Mumbai
(c) Bangkok
(d) Singapore

16 The 12th major port of the century, likely to be commissioned in 2001, is being constructed at

(a) Ennore
(b) Janput
(c) Tondi
(d) Nagore

17 Darjeeling Himalayan Railway (DHR) connecting New Jalpaiguri with Darjeeling has been declared as a world Heritage site. DHR is still operational and was opened in the year

(a) 1861
(b) 1871
(c) 1881

(d) 1891

18 Which among the following pairs of athletes were named 'Athletes of the Year 2000' by International Amateur Athletic Federation?
(a) Heike Drechsler & Marion Jones
(b) Jan Zelezny & Marion Jones
(c) C. J. Hunter & Mari On Jones
(d) Jan Zelezny & Cathy Freeman

19 India's first Naval Museum is expected to be commissioned by the end of January 2001. It is being built in which os the following cities?
(a) Kochi
(b) Vishakhpatnam
(c) Chennai
(d) Calcutta

20 In its 52nd session, UN General Assembly has declared the year 2001 as
(a) International Year of Volunteers
(b) International Year of Environment
(c) International Year for Eradication of AIDS
(d) International Year for Post and Telegraph

21 Armed Forces Flag Day is observed on
(a) 2nd December
(b) 7th December
(c) 9th December
(d) 12th December

22 How many adolescent girls are expected to be benefitted by the *Kishori Shakti Yojna* Launched by the Department of Women and Child Development, Ministry of Human Resources Development?
(a) 8 Lakh
(b) 10.08 Lakh
(c) 12.8 Lakh
(d) 15.80 Lakh

23 As per the estimates of the National Association of Software and Service Companies (NASSCOM), Indian domestic software market is expected to earn how much revenue in the year 2000-01 and 2001-02 respectively (in crore)?
(a) Rs 8000 & Rs 11000

(b) Rs 11000 & Rs 16000
(c) Rs 16000 & Rs 20000
(d) Rs 20000 & Rs 24000

24 International Folk Dance Festival was held during December 2000 at which of the following places?
(a) Nagpur
(b) Baroda
(c) Ahmedabad
(d) Jaipur

25 Alongwith Anil Kumble who among the following was selected for the K. K. Birla Foundation Award for Sports for the year 1999-2000?
(a) Shiny Walson
(b) Dhanraj Pillay
(c) Aarthie Ramaswamy
(d) Rahul Dravid

26 An hour-long interview with Pakistan military director General Pervez Musharraf by a journalist won him the 2000 Best Current Affairs Special Programme prize at Asian Television Awards in Singapore. Who among the following took this interview?
(a) Karan Thapar
(b) Pranoy Roy
(c) Vikram Chandra
(d) Barkha Dutt

27 Bank of Madura will be merged with which of the following financially & technologically strong banks?
(a) IDBI Bank
(b) ICICI Bank Ltd.
(c) Canara Bank
(d) HDFC Bank

28 Who among the following is a member of the Advisory Board of the United Nations Conference on Trade and Development and the Advisory Council of Jurists of the Asia-Pacific Forum of National Human Rights Institutions and was also fecilitated in December 2000 for completing 50 years of the Bar?
(a) Fali S. Nariman
(b) Rajesh Verma

(c) Syed Ali Shah
(d) Samir Dey

29 The 50th General Assembly and World Congress of International Press Institute is scheduled to be held in which of the following cities in January 2001?
(a) Kolkata
(b) New Delhi
(c) Singapore
(d) Colombo

30 The novel 'Pahla Girmitya' has been selected for the prestigious annual literary award Vyas Samman for the year 2000. Who among the following wrote it?
(a) Giriraj Kishore
(b) Harish Salve
(c) Gopichand Mishra
(d) S. Gupta

31 Who among the following Gupta kings stopped the Huns of Central Asia from invading India?
(a) Samudragupta
(b) Skandgupta
(c) Kumargupta
(d) Chandragupta

32 In which of the following major temples in South India, Shiva is worshipped as Nataraja or 'Lord of the Dance' instead of Lingam?
(a) Bihadeeshwara temple
(b) Meenakshi temple
(c) Pandyas temple
(d) Chidambaram temple

33 Who among the following demarcated the line which divides India and Pakistan?
(a) Sir Mortimer Durand
(b) Sir Henary McMohan
(c) Lord Mountbatten
(d) Sir Cyril Radcliff

34 Who among the following British Governor-Generals introduced postage stamps in India?
(a) Lord Aukland

(b) Lord William Bentinck
(c) Lord Dalhousie
(d) Lord Canning

35 Who among the following has written the book 'Thought on Pakistan'?
(a) Abul Kalam Azad
(b) B. R. Ambedkar
(c) Bal Gangadhar Tilak
(d) Jawaharlal Nehru

36 IRDA has issued six licences with 26 percent foreign equity to launch general insurance business in India. Among who the six companies granted licence, which of the following companies does not have a foreign partner?
(a) IFFCO
(b) ICICI
(c) Reliance
(d) HDFC

37 A 116-year old General Post Office building built in Indo-Saracenic style was gutted in a major fire in October 2000. In which of the following cities it is located?
(a) Chennai
(b) Kolkata
(c) New Delhi
(d) Bangalore

38 Who among the following is the Chairman of the Central Board of Direct Taxes?
(a) A. Balasubramaniam
(b) Arun Arora
(c) P. S. Subramaniam
(d) Ramesh Chandra

39 In which of the following cities an International Animation Film Festival was inaugurated during October 2000?
(a) Tjiruvananthapuram
(b) Bangalore
(c) Mumbai
(d) Hyderabad

40 2006 Asian Games are scheduled to held in

(a) Hong Kong
(b) Kuala Lalampur
(c) Doha
(d) New Delhi

41 At present, who among the following is the United Kingdom's High Commissioner to India?
(a) Patricia Hewitt
(b) Sir Rob Young
(c) N. R. Robinson
(d) Victor Joy

42 34th Chess Olympiad was played during October-November 2000 in which of the following cities?
(a) Istanbul
(b) Chennai
(c) London
(d) Paris

43 Which of the following is not the highlight of the Direct-To-Home broadcasting cleared by the government?
(a) Separate licences for Internet, fax services on DTH
(b) Recording of programmes to be preserved for 120 days
(c) Only 20% foreign direct investment
(d) Ten percent government share in annual profits

44 While formulating the New Textile Policy in the year 2000, government accepted all the recommendations which of the following committee?
(a) Kashiram Committee
(b) Satyam Committee
(c) Abdullah Committee
(d) Bhattacharya Committee

45 Who among the following is the Director of Research Foundation for Science Technology and Ecology?
(a) Vandana Shiva
(b) Sushma Swaraj
(c) Viren Shah
(d) Vandana Saha

46 Parliament has frozen fresh delimitation of Assembly Constituencies all over the country till the year 2026. Which of the following States

has become an exception and Election Commission is setting up new section to carry out this task?
(a) Chhattisgarh
(b) Jharkhand
(c) Uttaranchal
(d) Sikkim

47 Which of the following is the name of India's indigenously built Unmanned Air Vehicle (UAV) designed for aerial battlefield reconnaissance including target acquisition?
(a) Vajra
(b) Lakshya
(c) Baaz
(d) Surya

48 Eighth General Assembly of the Asia-Pacefic Parliamentarians' Conference on Environment and Development was held during November 2000 at which of the following cities?
(a) Hyderabad
(b) Singapore
(c) Bangkok
(d) Bangalore

49 Pandit Bhimsen Joshi, selected for the 5th Aditya Birla Kalashikhar Puruskar in the field of 'Hindustani Classical Vocal', is from which of the following Gharanas?
(a) Kirana
(b) Agri
(c) Gwalior
(d) Nirana

50 Who among the following is the elected member of the United Nations Committee which decides on the contentious issue of contribution by member states to the world body?
(a) C. R. Garekhan
(b) P. C. Alexander
(c) M. M. Jacob
(d) P. Radhkrishnan

51 World Cup Carrom Championship was held during November 2000 in which of the following cities?
(a) Chennai

(b) Mumbai
(c) New Delhi
(d) Bangalore

52 800 MW Kal Dam Hydro-electric Project is being built in which of the following States?
(a) Jammu & Kashmir
(b) Himachal Pradesh
(c) Uttaranchal
(d) Tamil Nadu

53 During the last 25 years, NTPC has operated 12 coal-based and seven gas-based plants and has achieved a generating capacity of
(a) 16435 MW
(b) 19435 MW
(c) 25435 MW
(d) 28435 MW

54 Sonal Mansingh is the exponent of which of the following dance forms?
(a) Odissi
(b) Yakshagana
(c) Manipuri
(d) Kuchipudi

55 The booker Prize winner for 2000, Margarate Atwood has written which of the following books?
(a) The Blind Assassin
(b) Survival
(c) Life Before Man
(d) All of these

56 During the first-half of the financial year 2000-01, software industry of India has generated a revenue of how many crores?
(a) Rs. 11,150
(b) Rs. 17,150
(c) Rs. 21,150
(d) Rs. 25,150

57 New York-based Chatterjee Group has tied up with German firm BASF, AG Ludwigshafen, for manufacturing polystyrene in India through a joint venture, at which of the following places?
(a) Dahej (Gujarat)

(b) Haldia (West Bengal)
(c) Panvel (Mumbai)
(d) Tumkur (Karnataka)

58 Which of the following countries is not a participant to the Mekong-Ganga Cooperation?
(a) Vietnam
(b) Myanmar
(c) Cambodia
(d) Sri Lanka

59 Which among the following teams won the Durand Cup 2000?
(a) East Bengal
(b) Mahindra United
(c) Mohun Bagan
(d) Railways

60 Ringo Starr, George Harrison and Paul McCartney were in the news during October 2000 on account of release of new book which recounts their story from childhood. They were associated with which groups?
(a) Beatles
(b) Starship
(c) Eagles
(d) Pink Floyed

61 Who among the following is the Director of CIA, who was in the news for release of five million pages of declassified intelligence documents in Washington, USA?
(a) Jacques Rogge
(b) George Tenet
(c) Victor Conet
(d) Paul Scholas

62 ICICI Ltd. has entered into a joint venture with which of the following companies to launch general insurance business in India?
(a) American International Group
(b) STC (USA)
(c) Lambard (Canada)
(d) Lowe Lintas (India)

63 Who among the following is the present National Champion for Women's Snooker in India?

(a) Varsha Mazumdar
(b) Neeta Sanghvi
(c) Pooja Gulundia
(d) Judith Walia

64 Who among the following won the historic Presidential elections held in Yugoslavia in September 2000?
(a) Slobodon Milosevic
(b) Vajislav Kostunica
(c) Vajislav Milosevic
(d) Mirka Marjanovic

65 Wembley Stadium in London was in the news during October 2000, for which of the following reasons?
(a) Live Aid Famine Relief concert was held here in October 2000
(b) It has been planned to be demolished
(c) India International show was held here in October 2000
(d) An aircraft of the Blue Angles, the US Navy's flying team, crashed here

66 The famous 'Bengal Army', which revolted against the Britishers in 1857 and subsequently disbanded, was actually recruited from a princely State away from Bengal. Which was this state?
(a) Jaipur
(b) Hyderabad
(c) Bundelkhand
(d) Oudh

67 Just before the release, which product's ad line was 'It is hot. It is coming'?
(a) Corsa
(b) Accent
(c) Alto
(d) City VTEC

68 The book 'The Magic of Malgudi' comprises three novels by R. K. Narayan, each depicting a stage in a man's life. Which of the following is not among these three?
(a) Swami and Friends
(b) The Tunnel of Time
(c) The Vendor of Sweets
(d) The Bachelor of Arts

69 Who among the following was the chief prosecutor of Edwin King Commission (South Africa) who visited India, concerning the Cricket match-fixing scandal, in September 2000?
(a) Shamila Batohi
(b) Sangeeta Batohi
(c) Preeti Mbeki
(d) Shamila Muluzi

70 Trajon Horses and Logic Bombs are associated with
(a) War Bombs
(b) Internet Hacking
(c) Modern Toys
(d) Computer Games

71 Who among the following heads the Commission of Inquiry set up by the Centre to hold a fresh probe into 1984 anti Sikh riots?
(a) Justice G. T. Nanavati
(b) Justice N. Gopalaswamy
(c) Justice Bishwanath Agarwal
(d) Justice Brijesh Kumar

72 Who among the following is Grasim Mr. International 2000?
(a) Anshuman Swami
(b) Aryan Vaid
(c) Rishi Prassad
(d) Vinod Chopra

73 Which of the following is an International hit series created by Ragdoll Ltd., which has been aired in over 120 countries and in 35 languages and is being telecast on DD Metro?
(a) Tintin
(b) Tintubbies
(c) Teletubbies
(d) Little Lester

74 Who among the following holds the record of the highest individual score by an Indian while batting for the first time in a One-Dayer?
(a) Brijesh Patel
(b) Navjot Sidhu
(c) Ajit Wadekar
(d) Yuvraj Singh

75 Under which section of the Representation of People's Act, anyone who is sentenced to more than two years in jail is debarred from contesting elections for six years from the date of conviction?
(a) Section 8 (3) (A)
(b) Section 16 (3) (A)
(c) Section 24 (3) (A)
(d) Section 32 (3) (A)

76 Who among the following was conferred the Indira Gandhi Award for National Integration for 1999 in October 2000?
(a) Rahul Dhawan
(b) Satish Dhawan
(c) Krishna Kant
(d) Suraj Bhan

77 'Kid A', 'The Blends' and 'Ok Computer' are the music albums of which band in UK, also known for their anti-consumerist stance?
(a) Radioband
(b) Boston Symphony
(c) Orange
(d) Pinkhead

78 Three researchers have shared the 2000 Nobel Prize for Physics. Who among the following is not one of them?
(a) Jack Kilby
(b) Zhores I Alferov
(c) Herbert Kroemer
(d) Alan Heeger

79 1080 MW Bhadrawati Coal-fired Power Project is scheduled to be set up in
(a) Madhya Pradesh
(b) Andhra Pradesh
(c) Maharashtra
(d) Orissa

80 Who among the following was conferred fifth 2000 Nobel Peace Prize?
(a) Kim Hee-Sang
(b) Kim Dae-Jung
(c) Kim II Chol
(d) Hong Song Nam

81 World Tourism Day was observed on
(a) September 16
(b) September 22
(c) September 27
(d) September 30

82 India Internet World 2000 Expo was held in September 2000 in
(a) Mumbai
(b) Bangalore
(c) New delhi
(d) Hyderabad

83 Which of the following is not among the three financial institutions that have bought part of 50 percent share in the Indraprastha Gas Ltd., jointly promoted by GAIL and BPCL?
(a) Unit Trust of India
(b) ICICI
(c) IL & FS
(d) IDFC

84 Bharat Sanchar Nigam Ltd., the country's largest ever Public Sector company, was born on October 1, 2000. Its head-quarters are at
(a) Dehradun
(b) Mumbai
(c) New Delhi
(d) Bangalore

85 Who among the following was the President of the Sydney 2000 Olympic Organisation Committee?
(a) Francois Carrard
(b) Michael Knight
(c) John Coates
(d) Sandy Haollway

86 During Sydney Olympics 2000, which country won the maximum number of medals?
(a) Japan
(b) Australia
(c) USA
(d) France

87 Which of the following countries did not figure among the first five in the final medals tally of the Sydney Olympic Games?

(a) France
(b) Germany
(c) Australia
(d) China

88 Who among the following ignited the Olympic flame at the Opening Ceremony of the Sydney Olympics?
(a) Ian Thorpe
(b) Cathy Freeman
(c) Daniel Igali
(d) Birgit Fischer

89 How many sports were played at the Sydney Olympics?
(a) 26
(b) 27
(c) 28
(d) 29

90 Which among the following was a new individual event introduced in the Sydney Olympics for men and women?
(a) Artitic Gymnastics
(b) Trampoline
(c) Rowing
(d) Taekwondo

91 A little girl and an aboriginal dancer Djakapurra Munyarryun were the two central characters who participated in the Opening Ceremony of the Sydney Olympic Games. What was the name of this little girl?
(a) Nikki Atkin
(b) Nikki Webster
(c) Tina Arena
(d) Nick Green

92 Three countries fielded their teams for the first time at the Sydney Olympics. Which among the following does not belong to this group?
(a) East Timor
(b) Rwanda
(c) Bosnia
(d) Cameroon

93 During the Opening Ceremony who among the following read the

oath on behalf of more than 10000 athletes at the Sydney Olympic Games?
(a) Rechelle Hawkes
(b) Andrew Gaze
(c) Cathy Freeman
(d) Chris Fydler

94 Who among the following was the flag-bearer leading the Indian contingent at the Sydney Olympic Games?
(a) Leander Paes
(b) K. M. Beenamol
(c) P. Gopichand
(d) Nisha Millet

95 Men's Olympic Football tournament was won by
(a) Spain
(b) Australia
(c) Cameroon
(d) Nigeria

96 Opening Ceremony, a four-hour extavaganza, was produced by whom among the following?
(a) Tina Arena
(b) John Coates
(c) Michael Wenden
(d) David Atkins

97 Who among the following was the chief of the Indian contingent to the Sydney Olympics
(a) Ashwin Kumar
(b) Ashok Mattoo
(c) P. S. M. Chander
(d) Mohd. Riaz

98 India was represented in Judo at the Sydney Olympics by
(a) Arijana Jaha
(b) Sanamacha Chanu
(c) L. Brojeshori Devi
(d) Vinita Tripathi

99 In which of the following team events, China's squad won the first Olympic team Gold medal in their nation's history?
(a) Women's gymnastics

(b) Men's gymnastics
(c) Equestrian men
(d) Fencing women

100 Which one of the following star athletes fled the Sydney Olympics after claiming that she had received threats to her safety at her hotel?
(a) Marie-Jose Pierce
(b) Marlene Ottey
(c) Peta-Gay Dawdie
(d) Gwen Tottence

101 India's bantamweight fighter and Bangkok Asian Games Gold medalist N. G. Dingko Singh was defeated by whom among the following?
(a) Kim Ki-Suk (South Korea)
(b) Sorgiy Danylchenko (Ukraine)
(c) Felix Savon (Cuba)
(d) Michael Bennett (USA)

102 Who among the following won the Women's Swimming 100m freestyle?
(a) Agnes Kovacs (Hungry)
(b) Jenny Thompson (USA)
(c) Inge de Bruijn (Netherlands)
(d) Kristy Kowal (USA)

103 Who among the following won the Olympic Men's Hockey title at the Sydney Olympic Games?
(a) South Korea
(b) Pakistan
(c) Australia
(d) Netherlands

104 Who among the following was not a member of the Women's 4 x 100 m Relay team of India for the Sydney Olympics?
(a) Rachita Mistry
(b) V. Jayalakshmi
(c) Vinita Tripathi
(d) Jincy Philip

105 Who among the following became the World's Sprint King & Queen after 100 m athletic event?

(a) Ato Boldon & Marion Jones
(b) Maurice Greene & Marian Jones
(c) Mourice Greene & Tanya Lawrence
(d) Ato Boldon & Jenny Thomson

106 Who among the following emerged as the greatest all-rounder female athlete at the Sydney Olymics?
(a) Denis Lewis (Britain)
(b) Marion Jones (USA)
(c) Naoko Takahashi (Japan)
(d) Joyce Chepchumba (Kenya)

107 Who among the following won the men's 10,000 m race at the Sydney Olympics?
(a) Paul Tergat (Kenya)
(b) Haile Gebrselassie (Ethiopia)
(c) Assefa Mezgebu (Ethiopia)
(d) Alvin Harrison (USA)

108 Who among the following won the Olymics Men's Tennis Gold medal at the Sydney Olympics?
(a) Tommy Haas (Germany)
(b) Arnaudde Pasquale (France)
(c) Yevgeny Kafelnikov (Russia)
(d) Sebastien Lareau (Canada)

109 Men's Marathon at the Sydney Olympic Games was won by
(a) Eric Wainaina (Kenya)
(b) Tesfaye Tala (Ethiopia)
(c) Genzahgne Abera (Ethiopia)
(d) Terry Brands (USA)

110 Who among the following won the all round Gold for Gymnastics at Sydney and later was found positive for the banned stimulant Pseudo-ephedrine?
(a) Yulia Barslukova
(b) Andrea Reduction
(c) Alina Kobaeva
(d) Yulia Raskina

111 U. S. dream team, which clinched the Gold medal, participated in which of the following events at the Sydney Olympics?
(a) 4x100 m Relay

(b) Basketball
(c) Water polo
(d) Equestrian

112 Imtiaz Aneez of India participated in which of the following events at the Sydney Olympics?
(a) Judo
(b) Swimming
(c) Equestrian
(d) Shooting

113 In the men's Double Tennis, Leander Paes and Mahesh Bhupati were defeated in the second round by
(a) Andrei Pavel & Gabriel Trifu
(b) Mark Woodforde & Andrei Pavel
(c) Mark Woodforde &Todd Woodbridge
(d) Michael Tillstrom & Todd Woodbridge

114 Which of the following countries won Olympic Men's Volleyball Gold for the first time?
(a) Slovakia
(b) Cuba
(c) Yugoslavia
(d) Turkey

115 On the second day of the Millennium World Peace Summit in New York, a group of women dominated the proceedings. Who among the following presided over this session?
(a) Betty Williams
(b) Jane Goodall
(c) Ela Gandhi
(d) Indu Jain

116 Which one of the following is not the highlight of the new policy approved by the government for Foreign Direct Investment in India?
(a) 100% FDI allowed on automatic route in internet, telecom infrastructure providers, e-mail and voice mail
(b) 5-8% royalty payment permitted to parent foreign companies by their wholly-owned subsidiaries operating in India
(c) Bharat Sanchar Nigam is formed and Telecom Department corporatisation is complete
(d) 10% royalty payment on foreign brand names and trade marks allowed

117 India's exports during April-July in the fiscal year 2000-01 grew at what rate compared to the corresponding period for 1999-2000?
(a) 22.53%
(b) 25.43%
(c) 28.53%
(d) 32.43%

118 Who among the following was award the 1999 Dada Saheb Phalke Award?
(a) Hrishikesh Mukharjee
(b) Yash Chopra
(c) Buddhadeb Dasgupta
(d) Rakesh Roshan

119 Who among the following is the Indian researcher who has shared World Food Prize 2000 with a Maxican Cereal Chemist for developing maize varieties with higher protein content?
(a) Rajender K. Bhattal
(b) Surinder K. Vasal
(c) Sharad K Verma
(d) Vidya Sagar Gupta

120 Netxcell.com, India's first m-business portal offering wireless access to the web from any hand-held device, has entered into an alliance with which of the following companies?
(a) Hughes
(b) Wipro Net Ltd.
(c) Infosys
(d) VSNL

121 Who among the following is the author of the first e-book, 'Riding The Bullet', released exclusively on Net?
(a) Naresh Gupta
(b) Stephen King
(c) George Sampaio
(d) Gyula Horn

122 According to the Reserve Bank of India's statistical supplement as on December 1, 2000, India's foreign exchange reserve stood (in billion dollors) at
(a) $ 38.02
(b) $ 35.02

(c) $ 39.02
(d) $ 40.02

123 Indbazaar.com tied up during August 2000 with which of the following leading financial market portals for high value commentary and analysis on the foreign exchange markets?
(a) freemarkets.com
(b) emecklai.com
(c) innodata.com
(d) diaspark.com

124 Who among the following is the author of the famous Harry Potter books?
(a) Maggie Smith
(b) J. K. Rowling
(c) Tatum O'Neal
(d) Mark Lester

125 What among the following was depicted on the medals for Sydney Olympics 2000 which apparently was being judged as a mistake?
(a) Roman Colosseum
(b) A Greek Temple
(c) Sydney Opera House
(d) Sydney Stadium

126 What among the following companies bagged the exclusive marketing rights on Doordarshan for the Sydney Olympics 2000?
(a) Synergy Communication Ltd.
(b) NDTV
(c) Pritish Nandy Communications Ltd.
(d) Roshan Communications Ltd.

127 Who among the following Bollywood stars is associated with Cygnus Publications and Communications, which has signed an agreement with ATN World?
(a) Mithun Chkraborty
(b) Rishi Kapoor
(c) Shah Rukh Khan
(d) Vinod Khanna

128 In a bid to expand its overseas consumer durables, BPL Ltd. is buying a CTV manufacturing facility in which of the following countries of Europe?

(a) Austria
(b) Switzerland
(c) Hungary
(d) Slovenia

129 Miss India (World) Priyanka Chopra was crowned Miss World 2000 on November 30, 2000 beating 94 other contestants. She is the ______ Indian to win the Miss World title.
(a) 2nd
(b) 3rd
(c) 4th
(d) 5th

130 On which of the following days is the National Sports Day celebrated in the memory of the legendary hockey wizard late Dhyan Chand
(a) August 24
(b) August 29
(c) September 8
(d) September 15

131 Which of the following companies is the first company in India to provide Internet access through General packet Radio Services (GPRS)?
(a) Airtel
(b) Reliance mobile
(c) BPL Mobile
(d) BT Cellnet

132 Which of the following is not among the four public sector companies put for strategic sale *en bloc* by the Cabinet Committee on Disinvestment?
(a) Hindustan Zinc Ltd.
(b) Hindustan Insecticide Ltd.
(c) Sponge Iron India Ltd.
(d) State Trading Corporation

133 Zee Telefilms Ltd. has joined hands with which of the following movie channels to provide Hollywood blockbusters to the Indian market?
(a) HBO
(b) TNT

(c) MGM
(d) Star TV

134 Who among the following is not the member of the 'legends only' club to have won four consecutive Gold Medals in the same individual event at Olympics?
(a) Paul Elvstrom (Denmark)
(b) Al Oerter (USA)
(c) Naim Suleymangolu (Turkey)
(d) Carl Lewis (USA)

135 Who among the following defeated the Thirteen Grand Slam-winner, Pete Sampras (USA) at the US Open 2000 in the Men's Singles final?
(a) Lleyton Hewitt
(b) Marat Safin
(c) Todd Martin
(d) Max Mirnyi

136 Who among the following is the Chief Minister of Jharkhand?
(a) V. C. Shukla
(b) Babulal Marandi
(c) Ajit Jogi
(d) Nityanand Swami

137 In terms of Purchasing Power Parity World Bank's annual World Development Report 1999 placed Indian economy as the
(a) Fourth Largest
(b) Fifth Largest
(c) Sixth Largest
(d) Seventh Largest

138 The present Pope went on a largest tour of which region in March 2000?
(a) Russia
(b) Greece
(c) Israel and Jordan
(d) Turkey

139 Which of the following States has the highest number of child labourers in the country?
(a) Bihar
(b) Uttar Pradesh

(c) Andhra Pradesh
(d) Madhya Pradesh

140 With reference to the new National Agricultural Policy announced by the government in July 2000, which of the following is not true?
(a) Price protection for farmers
(b) National Agricultural Insurance Scheme to be launched
(c) Over 4 percent annual growth rate
(d) Greater government sector participation through contract farming

141 Continuing the trend of mergers and acquisition (M&A) in IT sector, ICICI Infotech has acquired which of the following companies?
(a) Intouch Technologies
(b) Ecapital Solutions
(c) Rohan Software Pvt. Ltd.
(d) BFL Software

142 Standard Chartered Bank acquired which of the following banks to create the biggest and best international banking group in the Middle East and South Asia?
(a) ABN Amro Bank
(b) ANZ Grindleys Bank
(c) Bank of Japan
(d) Thailand Bank

143 Who among the following took over as the Army Chief in September 2000?
(a) Lt. Gen. Chandrashekhar Joshi
(b) Lt. Gen. H. M. Khanna
(c) Lt. Gen. Padmanabhan
(d) Lt. Gen. M. K. Sharma

144 Who was man of the match in the finals of the ICC knockout tournament held in Kenya in October 2000?
(a) Zaheer Khan
(b) Roger Twose
(c) Saurav Ganguli
(d) Chris Cairns

145 Satyam Infoways Ltd., an internet and e-commerce company, has entered into an agreement to acquire which of the following US-

based on-line mail?
(a) indiaplaza.com
(b) indya.com
(c) yahoo.com
(d) 123india.com

146 Who among the following was conferred the Magsaysay Award 2000 for government service?
(a) Atmakusumah Astraatmadja
(b) Liang Congjie
(c) Jesse Robredo
(d) Jockin Arputham

147 For the current financial year, 2000-01, Engineering Export Promotion Council has set up an export target of
(a) $ 4.3 billion
(b) $ 5.3 billion
(c) $ 5.9 billion
(d) $ 6.3 billion

148 Which of the following was/were the Sydney 2000 Olympic mascot(s)?
(a) Millie (the Echidna)
(b) Olly (the Kookaburra)
(c) Syd (the Platypus)
(d) All of these

149 What is the connection between the Rolling Stones hit 'Start me up' and computing?
(a) It was used at the launch of Windows 95
(b) It was used at the launch of Mouse for personal computers
(c) It was used at the launch of Wndows 2000
(d) None of these

150 Indira Gandhi Centre for Atomic Research is located at
(a) Mumbai
(b) Kolkata
(c) Kalpakkam
(d) Indore

151 Who was the Republican candidate for the US Presidential elections held in November 2000?
(a) George Bush Jr.

(b) Al Gore
(c) Ralph Nader
(d) Dick Cheney

152 Who among the following has been awarded the GM Modi Innovative Science and Technology Award for the year 2000 for his achievements in medical technology?
(a) Dr. M. S. Valiathan
(b) Dr. K. C. Sharma
(c) Dr. Gajapathi Raju
(d) Dr. B. L. Wadhera

153 The shareholders of three Tata Electric companies have approved the merger of which of the following companies with Tata Power, making it the largest private power company in the country?
(a) Andhra Valley & Tata Info
(b) Andhra Valley & Tata Hydro
(c) Tamil Valley & Tata Hydro
(d) Tata Valley & Tata Hydro

154 The submarine, 'Sindhushastra', equipped with deadly 'Klub' anti-ship cruise missiles was inducted into Indian Navy in July 2000. Which class of submarine is this?
(a) Gram
(b) Kilo
(c) Nino
(d) Crui

155 Rajiv Gandhi Sadbhavna Award for 1999 was given to which of the following?
(a) Sunil Dutt
(b) Lata Mangeshkar
(c) Ustad Bismillah Khan
(d) Dilip Kumar

156 Which of the following is not a partner in the Utkal Alumina joint venture?
(a) Indal
(b) Norsk Hydro
(c) Alcan
(d) BAL

157 After commutation of life sentence by President of India, 5 Latvians

involved in the 1995 Purulia armsdrop case were released from Presidency jail in Kolkata. Their sixth associate still in jail is

(a) Peter Bleach
(b) Kim davy
(c) Igor Moskvitin
(d) Yevgeny Antimenko

158 Which of the following products, Hrithik Roshan appears in advertisements?

(a) Pepsi
(b) Coca Cola
(c) MRF
(d) Maruti

159 During July 2000, under which section of the Indian Penal Code, Shiv Sena Chief Bal Thackeray was arrested by Dadar Police and produced before the Additional Chief Metropolitan Magistrate?

(a) 151 (a)
(b) 153 (a)
(c) 155 (b)
(d) 156 (a)

160 Who among the following is currently the chairperson of the National commission for Women?

(a) Hema Malini
(b) Vibha Parthasarthy
(c) Abha Sharma
(d) Mohini Giri

161 Name the small car launched by Maruti in September 2000

(a) Alfa
(b) Alto
(c) Matiz
(d) Golf

162 Bill Clinton was the fourth US President to visit India. Who was the last US President to visit India before Clinton

(a) D. Eisenhower
(b) John F. Cannedy
(c) Richard Nixon
(d) Jimmy Carter

163 India and five ASEAN states-Thailand, Myanmar, Vietnam, Laos

and Cambodia-have agreed to cooperate towards developing transportation infrastructure, human resources development and Science & Technology. This project is called
(a) Swarnabhoomi Project
(b) Ganga-Mekong Project
(c) Mekong-Ganga Cooperation
(d) None of these

164 World Chess Championship 2000 (men & women) was held in November/December in which of the following countries?
(a) India
(b) Russia
(c) Switzerland
(d) Holland

165 Euro 2000 Soccer Championships held in Rotterdam (The Netherlands) was won by
(a) Italy
(b) Holland
(c) France
(d) Portugal

166 1999 Arjuna Award winner Aashim Mongia is associated with which of the following games/sports?
(a) Volleyball
(b) Yatching
(c) Rowing
(d) Boxing

167 Which one of the following films was awarded the Best Feature Film at the 47th National Film Awards held on September 18, 2000?
(a) Vaanprastham
(b) Uttara (Bengali)
(c) Hey Ram (Hindi)
(d) Shaheed Udham Singh (Punjabi)

168 The export of engineering goods and service during the financial year 1999-2000 was approximately (in US$ billion)
(a) 4.08
(b) 4.61
(c) 4.91
(d) 5.08

169 World Junior Weightlifting Championship was held during July 2000 at

(a) Parague
(b) Madrid
(c) Vienna
(d) Lyons

170 Who among the following led the Indian Hockey team to Sydney 2000 Olympics?

(a) Dhanraj Pillai
(b) Mukesh Kumar
(c) Baljit Saini
(d) Ramandeep Singh

171 National Waterway Number 1 will be linking which of the following two cities?

(a) Allahabad-Haldia
(b) Agra-Patna
(c) Cochin-Salem
(d) Dibrugarh-Haldia

172 World Cup Cricket Tournament in 2003 & 2007 are scheduled to be held respectively in

(a) South Africa and West Indies
(b) West Indies and South Africa
(c) South Africa and Britain
(d) Austarlia and West Indies

173 At present, which of the following is NOT a member of the OPEC?

(a) Saudi Arabia
(b) Kuwait
(c) Gabon
(d) Iraq

174 Which private bank was taken over by HDFC?

(a) Times Bank
(b) Indian bank
(c) Commercial Bank of India
(d) Federal Bank

175 Who among the following won the Wimbledon 2000 Women's Singles title held in July?

(a) Serena Williams

(b) Venus Williams
(c) Lindsay Davenport
(d) Martina Hingis

176 Which one of the following is not among the major initiatives for development of Information Technology and Telecom infrastructure in the country announced by the Prime Minister, Mr. Atal Bihari Vajpayee in July 2000
(a) No sales tax and other State Taxes on IT sector for next three to five years
(b) End of VSNL monopoly on under-sea optical fibre connectivity for ISPs
(c) Partial deregulation of National Long Distance Operations before August 15, 2000
(d) Task force set up on human resource development in IT

177 In today's world of Technology, the WML is the abbreviated form of
(a) Wireless Markup-Language
(b) Wide Markup Language
(c) Wireless Makeup Line
(d) None of these

178 Shrine of Virgin Mary in Europe is popularly known as
(a) Black Mary
(b) Black Madona
(c) White Madona
(d) None of these

179 The Archbishop of Delhi, who was in the forefront against the attacks in Christians in various parts of the country, died in June 2000 when his car was involved in an accident in Poland. He was....
(a) Donald D'Souza
(b) Cyril Mar Baselios
(c) Alan De Lastic
(d) John Dayal

180 Who among the following is the President of International; Court of Justice?
(a) Al-Khasawnch
(b) Syed Pirzada
(c) Gilbert Guillaume
(d) Don Mckinnon

181 Who among the following is the President of the reconstituted Indira Gandhi National Centre For Arts (INGCA)
(a) P. V. Krishna Bhatt
(b) M. V. Kamath
(c) Sonia Gandhi
(d) L. M. Singhvi

182 Who among the following is the only bowler in cricket history who has taken 400 wickets both in Tests and One-day Internationals?
(a) Courtney Walsh
(b) Richard Hadlee
(b) Wasim Akram
(d) Kapil Dev

183 Which of the following is not a partner of the go4i.com portal launched in June 2000 in India?
(a) HDFC Bank
(b) ICICI Bank
(c) The Hindustan Times
(d) Big Tree Entertainment

184 Who among the following ran 400 metres in 51.21 seconds at an athletic meet in Kiev, Ukrain and bettered the 15-year old P. T. Usha's record of 51.61 seconds set in Canberra (Australia) in 1985?
(a) K. M. Beenamal
(c) C. K. Mariam
(c) M. Saramma
(d) K. C. Rosakutty

185 Indian School of Business, a unique venture of 23 of the world's most respectable corporations and two top ranking business schools- J. L. Kellogg Graduate School of management and the Wharton School, which will focus on T-commerce, is being set out on the outskirts of
(a) Bangalore
(b) New Delhi
(c) Chennai
(d) Hyderabad

186 International Day against Drug Abuse and Illicit Trafficking is observed on
(a) June 22

(b) June 26
(c) July 12
(d) July 22

187 Who among the following became the first and the only star from the Indian Cinema who was waxed at the famous Madame Tussaud's wax Museum in London?
(a) Dilip Kumar
(b) Shatrughna Sinha
(c) Amitabh Bachchan
(d) Shah Rukh Khan

188 At the first ever International Indian Film Awards in London, who among the following was voted as the Best Actress of the Year?

(a) Raveena Tandon
(b) Aishwarya Rai
(b) Sonali Bendre
(d) Madhuri Dixit

189 Who among the following heads the research team working on Human Genome Project in Britain?
(a) Dr. Michael Dexter
(b) Dr. John Sulston
(c) Dr. Andrew Hynes
(d) Dr. John Dexter

190 When did India won the last Gold medal in Hockey at the Olympic Games?
(a) 1992
(b) 1980
(c) 1964
(d) 1972

191 The Prime Minister of which of the following countries declared in June 2000 that 'The war against Eritrea has been accomplished in victory and all its territory occupied by enemy has been liberated'?
(a) Ethiopia
(b) Somalia
(c) Egypt
(d) Nigeria

192 Who is the President of Pakistan?

(a) Pervez Musharraf
(b) Rafiq Tarar
(c) Abdus Sattar
(d) Farooq Leghari

193 The Millennium World Peace Summit was held in which of the following cities during June 2000?
(a) New York
(b) Moscow
(c) Paris
(d) London

194 Which of the following days is celebrated as the World Environment Day?
(a) 2nd June
(b) 5th June
(c) 10th June
(d) 15th June

195 Which of the following Indians was the overall incharge of UN Peacekeeping Force at Sierra Leone prior to the appointment of Lt. Gen. Daniel Opande?
(a) Major-General V. K. Sharma
(b) Major-General S. K. Garg
(c) Major-General V. K. Jetly
(d) Major General R. K. Yadav

196 Which Key button is found on the top left corner of standard computer keyboard?
(a) Tab
(b) Caps Lock
(c) Delete
(d) Escape

197 Guru Jai Shankar Menon is associated with which of the following dance forms?
(a) Bharatnatyam
(b) Odissy
(c) Kathak
(d) Manipuri

198 Which of the Indian Boxer narrowly missed a medal at the 2000 Sydney Olympics?

(a) Gurucharan Singh
(b) N. G. Dingko Singh
(c) Shakti Singh
(d) M. P. Singh

199 The abbreviation 'UNCED' stands for
(a) United Nations Commission on Environmental Development
(b) United Nations Commission on Educational Development
(c) United Nations Conference on Desertification
(d) None of these

200 Name the State carved out of Madhya Pradesh after the Parliament passed the legislation earlier in 2000
(a) Uttaranchal
(b) Vananchal
(c) Vidarbha
(d) Chhattisgarh

201 The World Congress of the International Press Institute which held in January 2001 in
(a) Mumbai
(b) New Delhi
(c) Kolkata
(d) Chennai

202 During May 2000, IT giant Infosys Technologies Ltd. announced a tie up agreement with which of the following companies?
(a) Lucent Technologies (US)
(b) Quintessent Communications (US)
(c) ICO Global Communications (India)
(d) ITC Infotech Ltd. (UK)

203 Which of the following is not the name of new State carved out of the existing States?
(a) Vananchal
(b) Uttaranchal
(c) Jharkhand
(d) Chattisgarh

204 After the passage of Information Technology Bill by the Parliament, India becomes the only country in South Asia and second in Asia to frame a legislation for e-commerce and Internet. Which of the following is the first Asian country to do so?

(a) China
(b) Thailand
(c) Singapore
(d) Malaysia

205 Who among the following is the Chairman of the Central Board of Secondary Education?
(a) Prof. B. P. Khandelwal
(b) Mr. Ashok Ganguly
(c) Mr. S. R. Kidwai
(d) Prof. H. R. Mehta

206 The control of which city was the cause of the breakdown of talks between Israel and the Palestinians in October 2000?
(a) Nazerath
(b) Gaza
(c) Amman
(d) Jerusalem

207 Who among the following cricketers was appointed a goodwill ambassador by the UN International Drug Control Programme during May 2000?
(a) Kapil Dev
(b) Jimmy Amarnath
(c) Courtney Walsh
(d) Sunil Gavaskar

208 The film 'Dancer in the Dark' won the Golden Palm at the 2000 Cannes film festival. Who among the following is the director of this film?
(a) Wong Kar-Wai
(b) Pavel Loungines
(c) Lars Von Trier
(d) Samira Makhmalbaf

209 Who among the following was the Fiji's civil coup leader who held the Prime Minister and his cabinet colleagues as hostages in the Parliament on May 19, 2000?
(a) Sitiveni Rabuka
(b) George Speight
(c) Lt. Col. R. V. Volavola
(d) Commander Frank Bainimarama

210 During the year 1999-2000, India exported handicraft products worth (in Rs. crore)
(a) 5924
(b) 5058
(c) 6234
(d) 6950

211 'Interpreter of Maladies' is a collection of short stories written by
(a) K. P. S. Menon
(b) Amita Malik
(c) Jhumpa Lahiri
(d) Anita Desai

212 Who among the following is the President of Sinn Fein, the IRA's political ally?
(a) Gerry Adams
(b) Jeffery Donaldson
(c) Jerry Peeters
(d) Rubens Kohler

213 To which country did the nuclear submarine 'Kursk' belong which sank in August 2000 killing all the sailors on board?
(b) Russia
(b) Finland
(c) Sweden
(d) Norway

214 Who among the following is the President of the Global chip giant 'Intel Corporation' who visited India during may 2000?
(a) Dr. Craig R. Brown
(b) Dr. Craig R. Barrett
(c) Horst Kohlr
(d) Jeff Henley

215 United Nations declared which of the following years as 'International Year for Culture of Peace'?
(a) 2000
(b) 2001
(c) 2002
(d) 2003

216 World Athletic Championship during the year 2003 is scheduled to be held in which of the following cities?

(a) Edmonton
(b) Paris
(c) London
(d) New York

217 Killada Satyam, the famous dancer, who died during April 2000 was associated with which of the following?
(a) Kuchipudi
(b) Bharatnatayam
(c) Odissy
(d) Manipuri

218 Who among the following received the prestigious Holdighati National Award 2000 for his/her achievements is the field of journalism?
(a) Asghar Ali Engineer
(b) V. S. Naipul
(c) Malini Parthasarthy
(d) Vir Bhadra Mishra

219 Who among the following is the author of the famous book 'The Blue Bedspread"?
(a) Funso Siyejina
(b) Shauna Singh Baldurn
(c) Raj Kamal Jha
(d) Shashi Deshpande

220 Based on the recommendations of the task force on infrastructure, six domestic airports will be upgraded to international level. Which of the following is not amongst these six?
(a) Ahmedabad
(b) Goa
(c) Guwahati
(d) Jaipur

221 The Russian State Duma ratified US-Russian strategic nuclear arms reduction treaty (START II) in April 2000. This treaty cuts US and Russian nuclear warheads from 6000 to no more than 3500 on each side by the year
(a) 2003
(b) 2005
(c) 2007

(d) 2008

222 India defeated whom among the following to win the four-nation Hockey title held during April 2000 at Perth?
(a) Germany
(b) Australia
(c) Pakistan
(d) Holland

223 Beighton Cup is associated with which of the following games/ sports?
(a) Football
(b) Golf
(c) Hockey
(d) Cricket

224 How many overs were allowed *per side* in the inaugural 1975 Cricket World Cup?
(a) 50
(b) 60
(c) 25
(d) 40

225 On April 28, 2000, a fierce fire destroyed over 11,000 tonnes of ammunition worth Rs. 376 crore at which of the following Ordnance depots of the Indian Army?
(a) Gwalior
(b) Jaipur
(c) Bharatpur
(d) Secunderabad

226 India's Nilabh Shastri was conferred the Distinguished Teacher Award in April 2000 by which for the following Universities?
(a) University of Manchester
(b) University of California
(c) Berlin University
(d) Moscow University

227 In which of the following countries 530 members of UN Peace Keeping Force (including 32 from India) were captured by rebel forces in April-May, 2000?
(a) Kosovo
(b) East Timor

(c) Sierra Leone
(d) Zimbabwe

228 Which of the following players won the Monte-Carlo Master Series trophy in the tournament held in Monaco on April 23, 2000?
(a) Cedric Pioline
(b) Dominik Hrbaty
(c) Pete Sampras
(d) Andre Agassi

229 Who among the following was the first female wind surfer to make a solo 60-day crossing of the Atlantic Ocean?
(a) Neli Jankova
(b) Rapha'la Le Gouvello
(c) Svetlana Habirova
(d) Anne Oltenbrito

230 Which Indian writer won the Los Angeles Times Book Prize for fiction for his novel 'Freedom Song'?
(a) Jhumpa Lahiri
(b) Amit Chaudhuri
(c) Vikram Chandra
(d) Vikram Seth

231 In which of the following countries was Miss Universe 2000 contest held on May 13, 2000?
(a) Turkey
(b) Egypt
(c) Cyprus
(d) Greece

232 In which French city, known for Airbus plant, President K. R. Narayanan visited during his five-day visit to France in April 2000?
(a) Toulouse
(b) Avignon
(c) Marseilles
(d) Lyons

233 Which foreign cricketer has set up 'Udyan', a home for destitute children in Barrackpore (West Bengal)
(a) Hansie Cronje
(b) Shane Warne
(c) Steve Waugh

(d) Courtney Walsh

234 Which of the following two stock exchanges merged on May 3, 2000 to create a Pan-European bourse handling more than half the continent's shares and laying Foundation for a global equity market?
(a) London & Paris
(b) Paris & Frankfurt
(c) London & Frankfurt
(d) Warsaw & Brussels

235 Which of the following European countries has, on the pattern of US Green Card System, announced plans to issue Green card visas to Indian IT Specialists within six months effective 1st August 2000 to facilitate the stay of 20000 workers upto five years?
(a) France
(b) Netherlands
(c) Germany
(d) UK

236 As per Statistical Outline of India, 1999-2000, as against 3.4 doctors per 1000 population in Germany, the corresponding figure for India is only
(a) 0.5
(b) 0.1
(c) 0.4
(d) 1.8

237 To which State does Dr. Rajkumar, the film actor, kidnapped by Veerappan, belong ?
(a) Tamil Nadu
(b) Karnataka
(c) Kerala
(d) Andhra Pradesh

238 Which of the following States has won the Ranji Trophy for 2000?
(a) Hyderabad
(b) Karnataka
(c) Punjab
(d) Mumbai

239 Senior National Football Championship (Santosh Trophy) 2000 which was won by Maharashtra defeating Kerala was held at which

of the following places?
(a) Kolkata
(b) Mumbai
(c) Panaji
(d) Thrissur

240 Apart from Amit Chaudhuri, which other writer with an Indian connection, has won the prestigious Los Angeles Times Book Prize?
(a) Vikram Seth
(b) Arundhati Roy
(c) Rohinton Mistry
(d) Salman Rushdie

241 Which former editor of an Indian newspaper was conferred the International Press Institute's World Press Freedom Award?
(a) R. K. Mishra
(b) V. N. Narayanan
(c) H. K. Dua
(d) Arun Shourie

242 Who has claimed the 2000 World Heavy-weight Championship title?
(a) Lannox Lewis
(b) Michael Grant
(c) Dante Cane
(d) Ronny Weller

243 Which of the following countries won the South Asian Handball Championships held in Dhaka on May 2, 2000?
(a) India
(b) Sri Lanka
(c) Bangladesh
(d) Pakistan

244 The Asian Schools of Table Tennis Championships 2000 were held in Hong Kong from July 11-17, 2000. Which of the following countries hosted the Asian Schools Hockey Championships in the first week of October 2000?
(a) Malaysia
(b) Pakistan
(c) Uzbekistan
(d) India

245 According to 'World Development Indicators 2000', India with a GNP of $427 billion (1998) stood at ________ place in world ranking
(a) 16
(b) 11
(c) 9
(d) 23

246 Which of the Indian State has two capitals?
(a) Assam
(b) Maharashtra
(c) Jammu & Kashmir
(d) Sikkim

247 The birth centenary of Adi Shankaracharya fell on
(a) May 8, 2000
(b) December 12, 2000
(c) June 30, 2000
(d) August 11, 2000

248 During 1999-2000, India's food production was (in million tonnes)
(a) 203.0
(b) 201.05
(c) 199.2
(d) 205

249 When and at what time one billionth child was born in India?
(a) May 11, 2000 (5.05 a.m.)
(b) April 30, 2000 (11.10 a.m.)
(c) May 5, 2000 (10.30 a.m.)
(d) May 17, 2000 (0.0 hours)

250 Which is the only active volcano in India?
(a) Barren Island in the Andamans
(b) Jwala Mukhi in Himachal Pradesh
(c) Lakshadweep
(d) New Moore Island

251 While LoC (Line of Control) is between J&K and Pak-occupied Kashmir, between which of the following countries LAC (Line of Actual Control) stands?
(a) India and Myanmar
(b) Taliban and Northern Alliance-held Afghan areas

(c) India and China
(d) China and Tibet

252 When do Mother's day and International Family day fall?
(a) May 14, May 15
(b) June 10, June 11
(c) January 8, January 9
(d) December 29, December 30

253 Which of the following countries has won the finals of 2000 Junior Women's Asia Cup Hockey which concluded in Kualalampur on May 13, 2000?
(a) India
(b) South Korea
(c) Pakistan
(d) Malaysia

254 The number of participants in the Miss Universe 2000 was
(a) 69
(b) 79
(c) 89
(d) 49

255 Which of the following is NOT the highlight of the new Export-Import Policy announced by the government for the year 2000-01
(a) Quantitative restrictions on 714 items removed
(b) Special Economic Zones to be set up
(c) EPCG scheme extended to all sectors without threshold limit at 8 percent duty
(d) Duty free replenishment certificate scheme for over 5000 products introduced

256 Who was awarded the Dada Saheb Phalke Award for the year 2000?
(a) Shyam Benegal
(b) Mrinal Sen
(c) Hrishikesh Mukherjee
(d) Subhash Ghai

257 Indian exports grew by what percent during eleven months of the fiscal year 1999-2000?
(a) 8.1%
(b) 10.21%
(c) 11.12%

(d) 13.21%

258 Who among the following was conferred the Chameli Devi Jain Award for 1999?
(a) Ms. Barkha Dutt
(b) Ms. Sonia Verma
(c) Ms. Shobhana Bhartia
(d) Ms. Nandini Mehta

259 Which among is the following is the village in South Kashmir where 35 Sikhs were massacred by Pakistan-backed militants on March 20, 2000?
(a) Bandipura
(b) Kokarnag
(c) Ranbir Singhpura
(d) Chatti Singhpura

260 Who among the following was selected for the K. K. Birla Award for Sports for the year 1999-2000?
(a) Dhanraj Pillai & Anuradha Biswal
(b) Jyothirmoyee Sikdar & P. T. Usha
(c) Anil Kumble & Arthi Ramaswamy
(d) Dhanraj Pallai & P. T. Usha

261 Nasi I and Nasi II Isles on the Gahirmatha coast in Kendrapara district of Orissa were in the news during March 2000 for which of the following reasons?
(a) Thousands of Olive Ridley sea turtles arrived here for nesting
(b) These islands were hit by super cyclone
(c) Master control facility for tracking INSAT-3B was set up here
(d) None of these

262 Who among the following was the captain of the 16-member Indian team that participated in the Sydney Olympics women's hockey qualifying tournament in Milton Keynes, England during March-April 2000?
(a) Helen Mary
(b) Ferdeen Ekka
(c) Tingongleima Chanu
(d) Amandeep Kaur

263 Who among the following is the exponent of Rudra Veena?
(a) Ustad Asad Ali Khan

(b) Ustad H. Sayeeduddin Dagar
(c) Pandit Vidur Mallick
(d) Pandit Hari Mohan Sharma

264 Who among the following was the recipient of 1999 Aditya Vikram Birla Kalashikhar Puruskar for his life time achievement in Hindustani Classical instrumental music?
(a) Pandit Ronu Majumdar
(b) Aneesh Pradhan
(c) Pandit Ram Narayan
(d) Pandit Tolaram Sharma

265 Who among the following is the Chief Minister of Pondichery?
(a) V. Vaithailingam
(b) P. Shanamugham
(c) P. Rangasamy
(d) R. V. Janakiraman

266 Who among the following was the winner of the men's singles title at the French Open Badminton Championship held during March 2000 in Paris?
(a) Jacek Niedzwiecki (Poland)
(b) Pavel Mecar (Slovakia)
(c) Chetan Anand (India)
(d) Siddarth Jain

267 INSAT Master Control facility is located at
(a) Hassan
(b) Thumba
(c) Ahmedabad
(d) Cochin

268 In one of the largest cash acquisition deals ever, Aditya Birla Group's Hindalco Industries Ltd. acquired share holdings of which of the following companies?
(a) INDAL
(b) BSES
(c) Escorts
(d) ITC

269 The 1999 Shankar Puruskar instituted by K. K. Birla Foundation was conferred for 'Sangeet Evam Chintan' on
(a) Dr. Prakash Agarwal

(b) Dr. Mukund Lath
(c) Dr. Hemant Joshi
(d) Dr. Mukul Seth

270 Which one of the following days is observed as the World Tuberculosis day?
(a) March 14
(b) March 21
(c) March 24
(d) April 12

271 Mr. Korst Koehler was in the news during March 2000 for which of the following reasons?
(a) He resigned as the IMF Chief
(b) He is the newly elected Chief of IMF
(c) He is newly elected Chief of WTO
(d) He was appointed as new President of Germany

272 Udham Singh, the second Indian to represented his country in four consecutive Olympics after Leslie Claudius, died in March 2000. He was associated with
(a) Athletics
(b) Hockey
(c) Weightlifting
(d) Shooting

273 What does IRA stands for
(a) Irish Republic Army
(b) Irish Republican Association
(c) Independent Republic's Army
(d) Inshue Republican Army

274 The Awards for Best Actor and Best Actress at the 72nd Academy Awards function held during March 2000 were given to
(a) Russel Crowe & Janet McTeer
(b) Kevin Spacey & Hillary Swank
(c) Sean Penn & Hillary Swank
(d) Richard Farnsworth & Meryl Streep

275 Who among the following is the leading wicket-taker in Test Cricket?
(a) Richard Hadlee
(b) Kapil Dev

(c) Wasim Akram
(d) Courtney Walsh

276 'Indian Women' is a book written by
(a) Anita Arya
(b) Asha Sharma
(c) Shashi Deshpande
(d) Ashok Desai

277 What is the name of the next generation super computer developed by the Centre for Development of Advanced Computing (C-DAC)?
(a) Param Anant
(b) Param Arjun
(c) Param Aditya
(d) Param Vijay

278 Tania Sachdev, V. K. Sindhu and Abhijeet Gupta are associated with which of the following games/sports?
(a) Swimming
(b) Shooting
(c) Chess
(d) Table Tennis

279 World Athletic Championship in 2001 is scheduled to be held in
(a) Edmonton
(b) Paris
(c) London
(d) Lisbon

280 Which one of the following is not the highlight of the Railway Budget for the financial year 2000-01?
(a) 7 percent increase in scale rates of parcels and luggage
(b) General 5 percent increase in freight rates
(c) No increase in passenger fares
(d) 25 new trains to be introduced

281 Who among the following is the Chairman of the Law Commission?
(a) Justice B. P. Jeevan Reddy
(b) Justice M. C. Sabharwal
(c) Justice Mohammed Shamim
(d) Justice J. S. Verma

282 Which of the following was not the highlight of the Economic Survey for the financial year 1999-2000?

(a) FDI inflows decline by 25 percent
(b) Agriculture production declines by 2.2 percent
(c) PSU disinvestments mop up 5,000 crore against a target of Rs. 10,000 crore
(d) Industrial growth rate pegged at 6.9 percent

283 Who among the following were selected jointly for the 35th Jnanpith Award for 1999 in March 2000?
(a) Nirmal Verma & Sunil Mukhi
(b) Gurdial Singh & Ganesh Prasad
(c) Nirmal Verma & Gurdial Singh
(d) Ganesh Prasad & Nirmal Verma

284 Tenth United Nations Conference on Trade and Development (UNCTAD) was held during February 2000 at
(a) Singapore
(b) Manila
(c) Bangkok
(d) Kualalampur

285 'Note Book of Foot Soldier' is a book written by whom among the following Indian authors who is also the Indian contender this year for a Commonwealth Writers Prize for the best book?
(a) Salman Rushdie
(b) Vikram Seth
(c) Randhir Khare
(d) Githa Hariharan

286 Slobodan Milosevic, the Yugoslav leader who was forced to step down in October 2000 was the President of
(a) Croatia
(b) Bosnia
(c) Slovania
(d) Serbia

287 ISRO's liquid propulsion system test centre complex is located at
(a) Mahendragiri (Tamil Nadu)
(b) Ahmedabad (Gujarat)
(c) Udaigiri (Orissa)
(d) Bangalore (Karnataka)

288 Who among the following was the Chairman of the five-member jury for the Commonwealth Writers Prize judged and awarded in

New Delhi on April 14, 2000?
(a) Shashi Deshpande
(b) Githa Hariharan
(c) Randhir Khare
(d) Girish Karnad

289 On October 1, 2000, the Government announced the formation of a new body with the Corporatisation of the Department of Telecom Operations (DTO) and Department of Telecom Services (DTS). What is the name of this new organisation?
(a) Videsh Sanchar Nigam Limited
(b) Bharat Sanchar Nigam Limited
(c) Mahanagar Telephones Nigam Limited
(d) Bharat Telephones Nigam Limited

290 A name 'Bariwali' (Lady of the House), which was in the news during February 2000, is
(a) The name of the Indian Bengali film that shared the NETPAC prize with Japanese film 'Nabbie No Koi' (Nobbie's Love) of the Berlin Film Festival
(b) The name of the most outstanding film in the Asia-Pacific, as declared at the Paris Film Festival
(c) The name of the film which bagged the Best Non-Feature Film Award at the 46th National Film Awards in February 2000
(d) None of these

291 Who among the following was the Chairman of the Kargil Committee?
(a) T. Krishnamurthy
(b) S. Sahini
(c) G. Sawant
(d) K. Subrahmaniyam

292 Sankhya Vahini, which was in the news during February 2000, is the
(a) High-speed submarine which can carry nuclear warheads
(b) High-speed (2.5 gegabytes per seconds) optical fibre data network which is designed to become a national data backbone of India
(c) High-speed rocket designed by ISRO
(d) None of these

293 Radhamohan Garanayak, who died in February 2000, was a noted

(a) Oriya poet and Sahitya Academy Award winner
(b) Bengali poet
(c) Odissy dancer
(d) None of these

294 Sultan Azlan Shah Hockey Tournament held during February 2000 at Kualalampur was won by
(a) Malaysia
(b) South Korea
(c) Pakistan
(d) India

295 India's oil import bill during fiscal 1999-2000 is estimated at
(a) Rs. 60,000
(b) Rs. 35,000
(c) Rs. 24,000
(d) Rs. 17,000

296 National Science Day is observed on
(a) February 15
(b) February 28
(c) March 5
(d) March 15

297 Who among the following has not been conferred the Visva Bharti's highest award 'Deshikottom' during February 2000?
(a) Shankha Chaudhury (Sculptor)
(b) Satish Gujral (Artist)
(c) V. Balsara (Musician)
(d) B. K. Ghosh (Film Director)

298 National Science award for Popularisation of Science was conferred in February 2000 on
(a) Dr. Yatish Aggarwal
(b) Prof. K. V. Keswan
(c) Prof. Lalima Verma
(d) Prof. K. T. Thomas

299 In the Union Budget 2000-01, Non-Plan Expenditure was increased by (Rs. in crore)
(a) 2395
(b) 8395
(c) 15693

(d) 17461

300 Which one of the following is not the highlight of the Union Budget 2000-01?

(a) Investment Ceilings of FII's in a company increased to 40 percent from 30 percent

(b) Dividend income being paid by the companies increased to 30 percent from 10 percent

(c) Tax on income distribution by debt oriented mutual funds hiked to 20 percent from 10 percent

(d) Minimum alternate tax (MAT) at 7.5 percent across the board, barring one exception

301 Which of the following is the largest mobile phone service company in the world?

(a) Telstra

(b) Airtouch

(c) Vodafone

(d) Novafone

302 During the first six months (April-September) of the fiscal year 2000-01, in dollor terms India's exports grew by

(a) 10.4%

(b) 22.4%

(c) 16.8%

(d) 18.2%

303 Who among the following became the Chief Minister of a State for the fifth time?

(a) W. Nipamacha Singh

(b) Naveen Patnaik

(c) Om Prakash Chautala

(d) Digvijay Singh

304 Inaugural Afro-Asian games are scheduled to be held in which of the following cities during November 2001?

(a) New Delhi

(b) Bangalore

(c) Pretoria

(d) Kinshasa

305 Who among the following is not the recipient of the Padma Vibhushan Award conferred on the eve of the Golden Jubilee of

the Republic Day?
(a) Radha Reddy (Art-Dance)
(b) Pandit Jasraj (Art-Classical Music-Vocal)
(c) Vilayat Khan (Art-Music-Instrumental)
(d) R. K. Narayan (Literature and Education)

306 On the Occasion of the 51st Republic Day, Ashok Chakra, the nation's highest peacetime gallantry award, was given posthumously to
(a) Lt. Col. Natraj Vijay Raghvan
(b) Maj. Sudhir Kumar
(c) Lt. Gen. H. M. Vij
(d) Col. B. S. Bhatnagar

307 An International Conference on Asian Security in the 21st Century was held in January 2000 at
(a) Bangkok
(b) Kathmandu
(c) New Delhi
(d) Colombo

308 Shubha Mudgal, Sita Nath Biswas and Sumitra Guha are associated with
(a) Dance
(b) Instrumental Music
(c) Hindustani Vocal Music
(d) Literature

309 International Custom day is observed on
(a) January 16
(b) January 24
(c) January 27
(d) January 28

310 Which one of the following committee gave its recommendation on badla under rolling settlement, set by the Securities and Exchange Board of India (SEBI) in December 1999?
(a) J. R. Verma Committee
(b) N. D. Tiwari Committee
(c) T. S. Krishna Committee
(d) None of these

311 'Harvesting Our Souls' is a book written by

(a) Pankaj Mishra
(b) Arun Shourie
(c) Shobha De
(d) Khushwant Singh

312 An International conference titled 'Magic International-2000' was held in January 2000 in which one of the following Indian cities?
(a) Hyderabad
(b) Nagpur
(c) Jaipur
(d) Udaipur

313 Which of the following is not a member of SAARC?
(a) Pakistan
(b) Nepal
(c) Bangladesh
(d) Afghanistan

314 The Ninth Asian Shooting Championship was held during January 2000 in
(a) Langkawi (Malaysia)
(b) Male (Maldives)
(c) Ratchaburi (Thailand)
(d) Surabaya (Indonesia)

315 Who among the following was the Chief Guest at the India's 51st Republic day celebrations
(a) Olusugan Obasanjo
(b) Ahmad Benbitour
(c) Shahabuddin Ahmed
(d) Gok Chok Tong

316 Shobhana Narain is associated with which of the following dance forms?
(a) Kathak
(b) Kuchipudi
(c) Manipuri
(d) Odissy

317 Mr. M. S. Verma was in the news during January 2000 for which of the following reasons?
(a) He was appointed Chairman of the UPSC
(b) He was appointed Chairman of the TRAI

(c) He was appointed Chairman of the Law Board
(d) None of these

318 Andre Agassi defeated who among the following in the men's final of the 2000 Australian Open?
(a) Ellis Ferreira
(b) Andrew Kratzminn
(c) Yevgeny Kafelnikov
(d) Magnus Norman

319 How much percent of government equity has been given to Hindustan Lever Limited for the management control of Modern Food Industries, a popular Public Sector bread manufacturer
(a) 51%
(b) 60%
(c) 69%
(d) 74%

320 Barring six areas, in most of the industrial sectors, 100% Foreign Direct Investment through automatic route has been allowed by the government. In which of the following sectors it is less than 100%
(a) In mining and prospecting of gold, silver, diamond and other minerals
(b) In coal and Ignite supply to private Indian power companies
(c) In Films
(d) In Advertising

321 As per the projection of the National Association of Software and Services, the Indian software industry during 1999-2000 is likely to earn how many billion US dollars?
(a) 5.1
(b) 5.7
(c) 6.2
(d) 6.5

322 Code name 'Springex' is associated with which of the following?
(a) Indian Navy's biggest ever war-games being conducted in the Arabian Sea.
(b) Name of the first International Fleet Review to be conducted by Indian Navy in Mumbai
(c) Name of the new software developed by Indian IT Professionals

(d) None of these

323 Who among the following has been appointed as the Chairman of the reconstituted research advisory committee?
(a) A. P. J. Abdul Kalam
(b) Montek S. Ahluwalia
(c) N. C. Saxena
(d) K. C. Pant

324 Ustad Alla Rakha Khan, representative of the Punjab Gharana who died in Mumbai on February 3, 2000, was associated with
(a) Tabla
(b) Sitar
(c) Flute
(d) Vocal Music

325 Who among the following was the creator of the oracle characters, The Hulk, Captain Marvel and Spiderman, and died in February 2000 at Miami?
(a) Gul Kane
(b) Marc Devic
(c) Marc Mundell
(d) Igor Sergeyev

326 Who among the following became the second Indian to receive the highest civilian award of France, "Commandeur de La Legion d'Honneur" in February 2000?
(a) Ravi Shankar
(b) Shiv Kumar Sharma
(c) Zakir Hussain
(d) Amajad Ali Khan

327 The Republican Party of the United States is also sometimes referred to as the GOP. What does GOP stands?
(a) Grand Old Party
(b) Government Opposition Party
(c) Grant's Old Party
(d) Great Oregon Party

328 Who among the following is not a member of the Constitution Review Commission constituted by the government in February, 2000?
(a) K. Parasran

(b) R. S. Sarkaria
(c) Subhash Kashyap
(d) R. K. Raghavan

329 At the 45th Filmfare Awards function in Mumbai, which among the following was declared as Best Actor & Best Actress?
(a) Shahrukh Khan & Aishwarya Rai
(b) Salman Khan & Madhuri Dixit
(c) Sanjay Dutt & Aishwarya Rai
(d) Anil Kapoor & Sushmita Sen

330 Assembly elections were held in February 2000 in which of the following States in India?
(a) Bihar, Orissa, Manipur and Haryana
(b) Bihar, Orissa, Manipur and Rajsthan
(c) Orissa, Andhra Pradesh, Goa and Haryana
(d) Kerala, Orissa, Haryana and Rajsthan

331 16th International Ramayana Conference was held during December 1999 in
(a) Kathmandu
(b) New Delhi
(c) Male
(d) London

332 Which of the following Indian newspaper celebrated its 75th anniversary on December 16, 1999?
(a) The Indian Express
(b) The Hindustan Times
(c) The Statesman
(d) The Economic Times

333 Who is the director of the film 'Mission Kashmir'?
(a) Ram Gopal Verma
(b) Vidhu Vinod Chopra
(c) E. Niwas
(d) Subhash Ghai

334 The recent Supreme Court judgement on the Sardar Sarovar Dam project on the Narmada river has allowed construction of the dam upto the height of
(a) 70 metres
(b) 90 metres

(c) 110 metres
(d) 138.6 metres

335 Which of the following South American countries was devastated by floods and mudslides in December 1999 killing more than 30,000 people?
(a) Colombia
(b) Peru
(c) Venenzuela
(d) Ecuador

336 In the finals of the National Squash Championship held during January 2000 in Chennai, men's and women's single title were won by respectively
(a) Manish Chotrani and Mekhala Subedar
(b) Manish Chotrani and Seepti Anvekar
(c) Ritwik Bhattacharya and Deepali Anvelar
(d) Bikram Uberoi and Mekhala Subedar

337 Name the former Congress party president who passed away in 2000?
(a) Sitaram Kesari
(b) Rajesh Pilot
(c) Rangarajan Kumarmanglam
(d) Ram Niwas Mirdha

338 Which State did the America buy from the Russia in 1867?
(a) Washington
(b) Hawaii
(c) Alaska
(d) California

339 87th Indian Science Congress was held during January 2000 at
(a) Pune
(b) Hyderabad
(c) Shimla
(d) Lucknow

340 Who among the following has been appointed as the new Davis Cup Non-Playing Captain of Indian team?
(a) Jaideep Mukherjee
(b) Ramesh Krishnan
(c) Anand Amritraj

(d) Mark Ferreira

341 The characters Bambi, Cinderella, Tinker Bell and Sleeping Beauty were created by whom among the following?
(a) Marc Andrew
(b) Marc Devic
(c) Eric Devis
(d) marc Mundell

342 'Speedpost' is the famous book written by
(a) Vikram Seth
(b) Khushwant Singh
(c) Shobha de
(d) Taslima Nasreen

343 In which of the following cities, IXth South Asian Federation Games are scheduled to be held in 2001?
(a) New Delhi
(b) Kathmandu
(c) Peshawar
(d) Colombo

344 In December 1999, the tiny enclave of Macau was transferred to China after 442 years. The enclave was under the rule of
(a) Britain
(b) Portugal
(c) France
(d) Japan

345 Who among the following won the men's single ATP Gold Flake Open tennis title at Chennai held during January 2000?
(a) Mark Hantschk
(b) Prahlad Srinath
(c) Julien Boutter
(d) Jerome Golmard

346 Vyas Samman for the year 1999 was awarded to
(a) Prof. Bhola Bhai Patel
(b) Dr. Sarkar K. Pal
(c) Shreelal Shukla
(d) Dr. Ajay Kumar Basu

347 During January 2002, in which of the following cities, the second World Cup Cricket for the Blind is scheduled to be held?

(a) New Delhi
(b) Christchurch
(c) Montreal
(d) Quebec

348 Who among the following received the 1998 Sanskriti Award for excellence in journalism?
(a) Praveen Swami
(b) Mohammed Aleem
(c) Anandajit Ray
(d) Anupam Seth

349 Who among the following received the 1998 Outstanding Parliamentarian Award?
(a) S. Jaipal Reddy
(b) Pranab Mukherjee
(c) Chandra Shekhar
(d) Indrajit Gupta

350 Asia Cup Cricket Tournament in 2001 will be hosted by
(a) Bangladesh
(b) Pakistan
(c) India
(d) Kathmandu

351 'Patterns of Destiny' is a novel written by
(a) Thakur Vijai Singh
(b) Andrew Miller
(c) R. K. Laxman
(d) Khushwant Singh

352 Who among the following is known as the architect of Indian missiles programme?
(a) Dr. A. P. J. Abdul Kalam
(b) K. Kasturirangam
(c) R. Chidamberam
(d) None of these

353 'RFSTE' is abbreviated form of
(a) Research Foundation for Science, Technology and Engineering
(b) Rural Foundation and Support for Technical Employment
(c) Rural Foundation for Science, Technology and Ecology
(d) Research Foundation for Science, technology and Ecology

354 Lok Sabha Speaker G. M. C. Balayogi was in the news during September 2000 for which of the following seasons?
(a) he has been elected to the Standing Committee of the South-east-Asian Speakers' and Presiding Officers' Conference
(b) he was unanimously elected as the "Asia Region Representative" of the Commonwealth Parliamentary association by 54-member general Assembly of the Commonwealth Parliamentary Association at Edinburgh (UK)
(c) He inaugurated the 35th session of the Indian Labour Conference
(d) None of these

355 India Economic Summit was held in November 2000 in
(a) Mumbai
(b) New Delhi
(c) Chennai
(d) Bangalore

356 The ninth G. D. Birla Award for Scientific Research for the year 1999 has been awarded to
(a) Dr. Sankar K. Oal
(b) Prof. Biman Bagchi
(c) Dr. S. S. Jha
(d) Prof. M. K. Bhan

357 In December 1999, Congentrix and China Light & Power Company withdrew from a fast track 1000 MW power project. This project was being built in the State of
(a) Andhra Pradesh
(b) Tamil Nadu
(c) Karnatak
(d) Kerala

358 Who among the following was selected for the prestigious Dr. Y. Nayudamma Memorial Award for 1999
(a) Dr. R. Chidambram
(b) Dr. D. Sengupta
(c) Mr. Ramesh Chandra
(d) Mr. N. Ravi

359 Who among the following was named in November 1999 as the "International man of the Year 2000" by the International

Biographical Centre, Cambridge, England?
(a) G. V. G. Krishnamurthy
(b) G. V. Ramkrishna
(c) C. S. Krishnamurthy
(d) Anil Sood

360 The second UN Economic and Social Commission for Asia and Pacific Ministerial Conference was held in November 1999 in
(a) Mumbai
(b) Colombo
(c) New Delhi
(d) Bangkok

361 Aneesh Pradhan, who was Awarded the Aditya Vikram Birla Kalakiran Purskar for the year 1999, is associated with
(a) Flute
(b) Tabla
(c) Sarangi
(d) Dance

362 Who among the following was awarded the 1999 Indira International Prize for Peace, Disarmament and Development
(a) M. S. Swaminathan
(b) A. Marchuk
(c) Robert Macnamara
(d) Prof. Mohammed Yunus

363 Arun Bajoria, a Calcutta-based businessmen, tried to take over which high profile company in 2000?
(a) Bombay Dyeing
(b) Telco
(c) Infosys
(d) Wipro

364 Who among the following was presented the 1999 Lal Bahadur Shastri International Award for Excellence in Academics and Management on September 30, 2000?
(a) Prof. C. K. Prahlad
(b) Salim Ahmed Salim
(c) Ms. Nafis Sadik
(d) Prof. C. S. Sharma

365 Mrs. Beatrix D'Souza and Mr. D. B. Atkinson were in the news in

November 1999 for which of the following reasons?
(a) They were nominated as member of the Rajya Sabha to represent Anglo-Indian Community
(b) They were nominated as representatives of the Anglo-Indian Community to the 13th Lok Sabha
(c) They were appointed Governors of Goa & Maharashtra respectively
(d) None of these

366 Who among the following was chosen as the Castrol Cricketer of the year 2000?
(a) Saurav Ganguly
(b) Anil Kumble
(c) Rahul Dravid
(d) Sachin Tendulkar

367 The abbreviation OSCE stands for
(a) Overseas Security and Cooperative Empire
(b) Organisation for Security and Cooperation in Europe
(c) Organisation for Security & Counter Exchange
(d) None of these

368 Who among the following was named 'Asian of the Century' by the 'Asiaweek' magician in December 1999?
(a) Akira Kurosawa
(b) Deng Xiaoping
(c) Mahatma Gandhi
(d) Charles Kao Kuen

369 Name the film directed by Manoj Shyamalan that was nominated for the Oscars 2000?
(a) Elizabeth
(b) The Sixth Sense
(c) Bombay Boys
(d) The Cell

370 International Day for Person with Disabilities was observed in 2000 on
(a) November 25
(b) December 3
(c) December 10
(d) December 12

371 Prof. M. N. Srinivas, who died in November, 1999, was an eminent
(a) Sociologist
(b) Economist
(c) Agriculturist
(d) Biologist

372 Who among the following was the Chairperson of the Third Ministerial Conference of the WTO held at Seattle in December 1999?
(a) Ms. Charlene Barshefsky
(b) Francisco Flores
(c) Jose Maria
(d) Ms. Jenny Shipley

373 Which country won the Hero Honda sponsored fourth Asia Cup Women's Hockey tournament held in December 1999?
(a) India
(b) China
(c) Malaysia
(d) South Korea

374 Who among the following was respectively named as the Best Male and Best Female Athletes of the Century by IAAF?
(a) Carl Lewis & Fenny Blankers-Koen
(b) Carl Lewis & Cathy Freeman
(c) Carl Lewis & Marie-Jose Perec
(d) Donovon Bailey & Fanny Blankers-Koen

375 Who among the following is the Chairman of the Planning Commission?
(a) A. B. Vajpayee
(b) K. C. Pant
(c) A. S. Dulat
(d) A. M. Khusro

376 'The Last Post' is a book written by
(a) S. K. Pachuri
(b) Narendar Pani
(c) P. C. Rao
(d) Ashok Beri

377 2051 MW Parvati Hydro-Electric Project, biggest of its kind in Asia, is being built in

(a) Haryana
(b) J & K
(c) Himachal Pradesh
(d) Uttar Pradesh

378 A trio of shiny horned creatures from outer space will be the mascots of the 2002 World Cup Soccer tournament, to be cohosted by South Korea and Japan. These fantasy figures are labelled as
(a) Etmos
(b) Atmol
(c) Atmos
(d) Atnob

379 First Winter South Asian Federation (SAF) Games were held in January-February 2000 in the cities of
(a) Shimla & Manali
(b) Shrinagar & Jammu
(c) Kathmandu & Pokhara
(d) Srinagar & Manali

380 Primo Nebiolo, the President of the International Amateur Athletics Federation, was in the news in November 1999 for which of the following reasons?
(a) He was re-elected for the fifth time in a row to be the President of IAAF
(b) He was elected to the powerful executive Olympic Committee
(c) He died in Rome at the age of 76
(d) None of these

381 World Post Day was observed on
(a) October 8
(b) October 9
(c) October 25
(d) November 9

382 Who among the following was elected as the President of Argentina in October 1999?
(a) Fernando de La Rua
(b) Zine Al-Abidine Ben Ali
(c) Carlos S. Menem
(d) Ahmed Ouyahia

383 Ms. Gargi parsi was in the news in October 1999 for which of the

following reasons?

(a) She has been awarded the Rajiv Gandhi Rashtriya Ekta Award for 1999

(b) She has been presented the World Food Day Award for 1999 for her contribution in raising public awareness about agriculture related issues

(c) She has been presented the Gurram Joshua Literary Award for 1998

(d) None of these

384 'Jaya Ganga', a much acclaimed and celebrated film, which was shown in 21 countries and at 28 film festivals, is based on a novel by

(a) Karan Singh

(b) Vijay Singh

(c) Baljit Singh

(d) Ajit Singh

385 Who among the following was not selected for the Swarna Jayanti fellowship for young scientists announced in 1999?

(a) Dr. Debajyoti Chaoudhury

(b) V. V. Ranade

(c) Umapathy

(d) Anurag Raghuvanshi

386 Pandit Satyadev Dube in associated with

(a) Dance

(b) Visual Arts

(c) Theatre

(d) None of these

387 How many squares are there on a standard chess board

(a) 48

(b) 64

(c) 100

(d) 96

388 Justice (Retd.) G. N. Ray Commission was set up to look into

(a) The Gaisal rail accident

(b) Effects of Killer Cyclone in Orissa

(c) Privatisation of Nationalised banks

(d) None of these

389 The annual Rath Marathon held in October 1999 in Jawaharlal Nehru Stadium, New Delhi was won in both men and women categories by respectively
(a) Heikam Ingoba Meetai and Rigzen Angmo
(b) Heikam Ingoba Meetai and Sharda Cahndel
(c) Durga Oraon and Rigzen Angmo
(d) Bala Ram and Mukti Roy

390 Who among the following was selected for the 1998 Dadasaheb Phalke award?
(a) Dev Anand
(b) B. R. Chopra
(c) Yash Chopra
(d) Ramanand Sagar

391 Who among the following is the Secratary-General of the Commonwealth ?
(a) Ervin Jose Arrieta
(b) Cesar Gaviria
(c) Todao Chino
(d) Don McKinnon

392 Who among the following is the Chairman of the Constitution Review panel?
(a) Justice M. N. Venkatachaliah
(b) Justice Shyam Sunder
(c) Justice D. Sengupta
(d) Justice P. B. Sawant

393 Who among the following is the ISI General whose appointment as the new Chief of Army Staff triggered off the coup in Pakistan?
(a) Lt. Gen. Khwaja Beg
(b) Lt. Gen. Khwaja Ziauddin
(c) Lt. Gen. Muhammad Haque
(d) Lt. Gen. K. M. Kasim

394 How many times has Atal Bihari Vajpayee been sworn in as the Prime Minister of India?
(a) One
(b) Two
(c) Three
(d) Four

395 The abbreviation 'INTERFET' stands for
(a) International Fund for Educational testing
(b) International Forum for European Trade
(c) International Force for East Timor
(d) None of these

396 The organistion "Medicines Sans Frontiers" was chosen for the 1999 Nobel Prize for Peace. Its headquarters are located at
(a) Paris
(b) Stockholm
(c) Rome
(d) Oslo

397 The book 'Letters between a father and son' is written by
(a) V. S. Naipaul
(b) S. S. Kohli
(c) N. A. Palkhivala
(d) Khushwant Singh

398 Loi Choa was defeated in October 1999 in a first ever boxing match between a man and a women. He was defeated by
(a) Margaret Shiny
(b) Margaret Macgregor
(c) Hong Jung-sung
(d) Renata Mauer

399 Tansen Samman for 2000, instituted by the Madhya Pradesh government for outstanding contribution to Hidustani classical music, is to be awarded to
(a) Ustad Ghulam Mustafa Khan
(b) Pandit Satya Dev Dube
(c) Pandit Jasraj
(d) Pandit Bhimsen Joshi

400 Which of the following countries was chosen to represent Asia as non-permanent member of the Security Council, for a two-year term starting from January 1, 2000?
(a) Sri Lanka
(b) India
(c) Bangladesh
(d) Thailand

401 What does ISP stands for?

(a) International Service Provider
(b) Indian Service Provider
(c) Internet Service Provider
(d) Internet Start-up Provider

402 The film 'Kairee invited to compete at the Festival of three Continents in Nantes (France) is directed by
(a) Adoor Gopalkrishnan
(b) Amol Palelkar
(c) Shyam Benegal
(d) Mahesh Bhatt

403 Padma Bhushan Raja and radha Reddy are associated with which of the following dance forms?
(a) Kuchipudi
(b) Kathakali
(c) Odissi
(d) Karragartam

404 Who among the following won the 1999 Gisela Bonn Award given by the Indian Council for Cultural Relations for promoting Indian culture?
(a) Hanna Paulmann
(b) Prafulla Desai
(c) Shawn Colvin
(d) Ela Bhatt

405 Who among the following created a record, in the general elections for the 13th Lok Sabha, by winning a Parliamentary seat for the tenth time in a row?
(a) Mufti Mohammad Sayeed
(b) Farooq Abdullah
(c) P. M. Sayeed
(d) K. P. Muthu Koya

406 The Pakistan Based Islamic militant group Harkat-Mujahideen (HUM) is also known by three other names. Find the odd group out.
(a) Al-Hadid
(b) Harkat-ul-Ansar
(c) Al-Jamah
(d) Al-Faran

407 Which Indian author narrowly missed Booker Prize for 1999?
(a) Namita Gokhale
(b) Anita Desai
(c) Vikram Seth
(d) Nayantara Sehgal

408 A killer super cyclone destructed large parts of which eastern State of India in 1999?
(a) Assam
(b) West Bengal
(c) Orissa
(d) Tamil Nadu

409 Who among the following is the Indian-American, who has been selected to share the Gandhi Peace Prize 2000 with Grameen Bank of Bangladesh
(a) Dr. Neeraj Kaushal
(b) Dr. Nelson Mandela
(c) Dr. Shailesh Verma
(d) Dr. A. Y. Garg

410 Which among the following political parties is not a member of the National Democratic Alliance led by A. B. Vajpayee?
(a) Trinamul Congress
(b) PMK
(c) MUL
(d) MGDK

411 Name the website which broke the Cricket match-fixing story in the year 2000?
(a) bazee.com
(b) tehelka.com
(c) tazaakhabar.com
(d) go4cricket.com

412 Who among the following received the Indira Gandhi Award for National Integration for the year 1998?
(a) Dr. Shankar Dayal Sharma
(b) K. R. Narayanan
(c) M. S. Gill
(d) G. V. G. Krishnamoorthy

413 Operation code-named 'White Sea' was used by Indian Air Force

in which of the following situations?
(a) To flush out extremists in Tripura
(b) to flush out Pakistani intruders from Kargil
(c) To chase the Indonesia forces as a member of the UN Peace Keeping Force in Dili
(d) To flush out LTTE members from territorial waters of India

414 The M. S. Verma Committee gave far-reaching recommendations on the
(a) Idle Gold Deposit Scheme
(b) Weak Banks
(c) Working of TRAI
(d) Working of MTNL

415 A. K. Pandian is associated with
(a) Weightlifting
(b) Volleyball
(c) Athletics
(d) Swimming

416 The first world chambers Congress, organised by the International Chamber of Congress, was held at
(a) Marseilles (France)
(b) Barcelona (Spain)
(c) Cologne (Austria)
(d) Salzburg

417 Almatti Dam which is being built over which of the following rivers?
(a) Cauvery
(b) Krishna
(c) Godavari
(d) Narmada

418 Which of the following countries was admitted as 190th member of the United Nations?
(a) Kiribati
(b) Nauru
(c) Tonga
(d) Yugoslavia

419 The International Day for the Preservation of Ozone Layer was observed on
(a) September 16

(b) September 25
(c) September 30
(d) October 5

420 The abbreviation 'PLOTE' stands for
(a) Prevalent Organisation for Trade & Economics
(b) People's Liberation Organisation of Tamil Eelam
(c) People's Liberation Organisation & its Transnational Encounters
(d) None of these

421 On September 24, 2000 and December 10, 2000, a countrywide mass immunisation programme was conducted for eradicating which of the following diseases?
(a) Leprosy
(b) Polio
(c) Chicken Pox
(d) Jaundice

422 The 2001 SAF Games are scheduled to be held at
(a) Peshawar
(b) Chennai
(c) Kandy
(d) Dhaka

423 Who among the following is the Director General of the International Olympic Committee?
(a) John Antonio Samaranch
(b) Jacques Diouf
(c) Wally N'Dow
(d) Nihal Rodrigo

424 Asian Shooting Championship was held in January 2000 at
(a) Lankavi
(b) Auckland
(c) Bangkok
(d) Ho Chi Minh City

425 'A Star Called Henry' and 'With Your Crooked Heart' are the two famous books. These are written respectively by
(a) Patricia Dunmore & Vikram Seth
(b) Reddy Doyale & Helen Dunmore
(c) Reddy Doyel & Salman Rushdie

(d) Helen Dunmore & Vikram Seth

426 RBI recently cleared the guidelines for launching Gold Deposit Scheme in the country. Which among the following is not one of its highlights?
(a) Incentive to banks by RBI/Government
(b) Maturity period to range from 2 to 5 years
(c) Banks to fix the initial lock-in period for the scheme
(d) Individual banks to fix interest rates

427 The World Tourism day was observed on
(a) September 27
(b) October 3
(c) October 12
(d) October 18

428 Who among the following is the first Indian to win a Formula 3 Car race?
(a) Hari Singh
(b) Narain Karthikeyan
(c) Uruguayan
(d) Ajit Singh

429 Ved Marwah was given additional charges as Governor of
(a) Meghalaya
(b) Mizoram
(c) Haryana
(d) Kerala

430 An eminent poetess, writer and artist Mrs. Vijaya Goel was in the news for which of the following reasons
(a) HRD Ministry presented her the national Award for the year 1998-99 for the Hindi fiction 'Kacchi Mitti Ke Log'
(b) She was appointed as governor of Kerala
(c) She was awarded Dr. Radhakrishnan Memorial National Teachers Award
(d) None of these

431 Andre Agassi defeated who among the following in the 1999 US Open Men's Single Tennis Championship?
(a) Pete Sampras
(b) Todd Martin
(c) Greg Rusedski

(d) Jared Palmer

432 The abbreviation 'html', widely used by internet users, stands for
(a) Hyper text mark up language
(b) Hyper text make up links
(c) Hot mail link
(d) None of these

433 The 600 MW Sawalkote hydro-electric Power Project is proposed to be located in which of the following States?
(a) Jammu & Kashmir
(b) Nagaland
(c) Assam
(d) Karnataka

434 Which one of the following films won the Best Feature Film Awards ceremony in September 2000?
(a) Hum Dil De Chuke Sanam
(b) Sarfarosh
(c) Shool
(d) Dr. Baba Saheb Ambedkar

435 The 13th Lok Sabha was constituted in
(a) 6th October
(b) 19th October
(c) 10th October
(d) 26th October

436 CACS (Capital Adequacy, Asset Quality, Compliance and System) is a new rating model announced by RBI. This system will be used to rate
(a) State-run banks outside India
(b) Foreign banks operating in India
(c) Private banks in India
(d) Cooperative Banks

437 "Fasting & Feasting" is a famous book written by
(a) Vikram Seth
(b) Anita desai
(c) Anita Brookner
(d) Salman Rushdie

438 Thirugnana Durai and Anand Menezes, are associated with
(a) Athletics

(b) Hockey
(c) Snooker
(d) Wrestling

439 Which Indian has the distinction of being the Vice President of World Bank?
(a) Dr. C. Rangrajan
(b) Dr. Bimal Jain
(c) P. Mankad
(d) Anil Sood

440 Inter-University Centre for Astronomy and Astrophysics is located at
(a) Pune
(b) Shimla
(c) Bangalore
(d) Kodaikanal

441 In which one of the Lok Sabha were not held in three phases?
(a) Andhra Pradesh
(b) Bihar
(c) Uttar Pradesh
(d) Rajasthan

442 Who among the following was given the 1999 Magsaysay Award for government service?
(a) Ms. Rosa Rosal (Philippines)
(b) Ms. Lin Hwai Min (Taiwan)
(c) Ms. Angela Gomes (Bnagladesh)
(d) Mr. Tasneem Ahmad Siddiqui (Pakistan)

443 Which of the following is the capital of East Timor which witnessed rampage by Indonesian troops and militants opposed to the territory's independence
(a) Dili
(b) Sutrana
(c) Ambon
(d) Tanimbar

444 Under which article of the Constitution, the Election Commission has been granted powers to superintend the election process in India?
(a) Article 126

(b) Article 32
(c) Article 324
(d) Article 97

445 Out of 543 seats for the 13th Lok sabha, how many seats have been reserved for scheduled castes and scheduled tribes respectively?
(a) 79 & 41
(b) 65 & 45
(c) 98 & 55
(d) 45 & 32

446 Seventh Athletics Championship was held during August, 1999 in which of the following countries?
(a) France
(b) Spain
(c) Germany
(d) Italy

447 Approximately 400 people were killed in head-on train collision in West Bengal during August, 1999. Name the place of the accident
(a) Gaisal
(b) New Jalpaiguri
(c) Siliguri
(d) Midnapore

448 Which of the following cities was rocked by a powerful earthquake measuring 7.1 on the Richter scale on August 17, 1999
(a) Ankara
(b) Istanbul
(c) Tunis
(d) Kampala

449 Eminent novelist Thakazhi Sivasankara Pillai was in the news for which of the following reasons?
(a) He was awarded the 1999 Jnanpith Award
(b) He died at the age of 87 at Thakazhi
(c) His novel 'Chemmeen' was released recently
(d) None of the above

450 In which of the following South-east Asian countries, about 830,000 pigs were executed in a battle to curb a viral epidemic (caused by Hendra Virus) that killed over 100 people?
(a) Malaysia

(b) Thailand
(c) The Philippines
(d) Cambodia

451 What is the name of India's most advanced satellite to date, which was successfully launched by an Ariane space vehicle at kourou in April 1999?
(a) INSAT - 2D
(b) INSAT - 2E
(c) INSAT - 2F
(d) IRS - 1E

452 Vazgen Sardsian who was shot dead in October, 1999 was the Prime Minister of
(a) Algeria
(b) Armenia
(c) Ethiopia
(d) Angola

453 What was codenamed as Trishul 99?
(a) It was the name of exercise to flush out the remaining terrorists from Jammu & Kashmir
(b) It was the name of the missile which will be launched during the middle of 1999
(c) It is the name of the three week long air exercise conducted along the northern borders of the country
(d) None of the above

454 Ms. Meghawati Sukarno was in the news for which of the following reasons?
(a) She has been elected President of Indonesia
(b) She is the Vice-President of Indonesia
(c) She was elected as Secretary-General of ASEAN
(d) None of the above

455 'Defending India' is a book written by
(a) Ramachandra Guha
(b) Harold Bloom
(c) Jaswant Singh
(d) Khushwant Singh

456 Diamond Jubilee Celebrations of the Indian Newspaper Society (INS) were inaugurated by President K. R. Narayanan during April

'99 in which of the following cities?
(a) Chennai
(b) Mumbai
(c) New Delhi
(d) Calcutta

457 The prestigious 4000-MW hirma Power Project is proposed to be set up in the State of
(a) Orissa
(b) Madhya Pradesh
(c) Punjab
(d) Rajsthan

458 The abbreviation RIPPT stands for
(a) Regional Investment Promotion and Protection Treaty
(b) Rural Investment Promotion and Protection Treaty
(c) Rashtriya Investment Promotion and Protection Transfer
(d) None of the above

459 Raja Rajeshwari and Rekha mal are associated with which of the following games/sports
(a) Shooting
(b) Powerlifting
(c) Table Tennis
(d) Golf

460 Who among the following were given the 1998 UNESCO peace prize?
(a) Sheikh Hasina Wajed and George Mitchell
(b) George Mitchell & Benjamin Netanyahu
(c) Benazir Bhutto & George Mitchell
(d) Chandrika Kumaratunga and Sheikh Hasina Wajed

461 World Tuberculosis Day was observed on
(a) March 21
(b) March 24
(c) March 29
(d) April 8

462 At the 72nd Academy Awards ceremony held on March 27, 2000 in Los Angeles, which of the following films won the maximum number of Oscars?
(a) The Cider House Rules

(b) Girl Interrupted
(c) American Beauty
(d) Boy's Don't Cry

463 Who among the following won the Oscar for the Best Director at the 72nd Academy Awards Ceremony?
(a) Sam Mendes
(b) Oliver Stone
(c) Manoj N. Shyaman
(d) Elia Kazan

464 2002 World Cup Men's Hockey tournament is scheduled to be held in
(a) Kuala Lumpur (Malaysia)
(b) Seoul (South Korea)
(c) Bonn (Germany)
(d) Manila (The Philippines)

465 Who among the following was elected as the first women President of SGPC?
(a) Ms. Harvinder Kaur
(b) Ms. Jaswinder Kaur
(c) Ms. Guldeep Kaur
(d) Ms. Jagir Kaur

466 Who among the following is the president of World Bank?
(a) Mitsuo Sato
(b) James Wolfensohn
(c) Michel Camdessus
(d) Rubens Ricupero

467 International Women's day is observed every year on
(a) February 28
(b) March 3
(c) March 5
(d) March 8

468 Which one of the following Commission of Inquiry was appointed by the Governor to Know the facts and circumstances relating to the killing of Mr. Graham Stewart Staimes and his two sons in January 1999 in village Manoharpur, Orissa?
(a) Justice Wadhwa Commission
(b) Justice Sharma Commission

(c) Justice Pillai Commission
(d) Justice Mishra Commission

469 'An Equal Music' and 'Ground Beneath Her Feet' are two books written by the respective Indian authors are
(a) Vikram Seth and Salman Rushdie
(b) Vikram Seth and Khushwant Singh
(c) Salman Rushdie and Mira Nair
(d) Salman Rushdie and Khushwant Singh

470 Who among the following is the recipient of 1999 Bharat Ratna posthumously?
(a) C. Subramaniam
(b) Ms. Aruna Asaf Ali
(c) Amartya Sen
(d) Gopinath Bordoloi

471 At the 44th filmfare Award Ceremony in February 1999, the Best Director Award was presented to
(a) J. P. Dutta
(b) Karan Johar
(c) Shekhar Kapur
(d) Aditya Chopra

472 The abbreviation 'CLIP' stands for
(a) Conference of Law in India and Pakistan
(b) Calling Line Indication Presentation
(c) Calling Line Image Presentation
(d) None of the above

473 As per the recent survey conducted by BBC, who among the following has been chosen as the Man of the Millennium?
(a) Mahatma Gandhi
(b) Winston Churchill
(c) William Shakespeare
(d) None of the above

474 Who among the following has been awarded 1998 Saraswati Samman, considered as one of the most prestigious literary honours in the country?
(a) Shankar Ghosh
(b) R. N. Dandekar
(c) Deepak Bannerjee

(d) Rajmal Devadas

475 The headquarters of National Coastal Zone Management Authority is at
(a) Mumbai
(b) Chennai
(c) Panaji
(d) New Delhi

476 United Nations declared the year 1999 as
(a) International Year of the Younger Persons
(b) International Year of the Older Persons
(c) International Year for Banning Chemical Weapons
(d) None of the above

477 Who among the following is the Chairman of the United News of India (UNI)?
(a) Arun Arora
(b) Narendra Sharma
(c) Ramesh Chandra
(d) Ashok Kumar

478 Who among the following women athletes won the Egyptian International Marathon held in February 1999?
(a) Karin Daheim (Germany)
(b) Karen Deorsa (USA)
(c) Sunita Rani (India)
(d) Rizon Agmo (India)

479 Dola Banerjee is associated with which of the following games/ sports?
(a) Archery
(b) Golf
(c) Table Tennis
(d) Athletics

480 During the National Award for the year 1999, who among the following was adjudged as the Best Sportswomen?
(a) Sreeja Majumdar
(b) Nisha Millet
(c) Tumpa Debnath
(d) Sapra Bin Moosa

481 G. D. Birla National Award for the year 1998 was presented to

(a) P. M. Udani
(b) Bharat Kumar Taparia
(c) K. P. Sharma
(d) Pandurang Shastri Athavale

997 Who among the following is *not* a table tennis player
(a) Kishan Maharaj
(b) Vijay Ghate
(c) Subhash Kamath
(d) Satish Vyas

483 Which among the following pairs won the 1999 Men's doubles Australian Open Championship?
(a) Patrik Rafter & Jonas Bjorkman
(b) Mahesh Bhupati & Leander Paes
(c) Ellis Ferreira & Rick Leach
(d) Todd Woodbridge & Mark Woodforde

484 Which of the following East Asian countries was rocked by a strong earthquake which killed more than 100 people?
(a) Japan
(b) Singapore
(c) Taiwan
(d) Philippines

485 Who among the following was the Chief Guest at the 1999 Republic day function?
(a) King Birendra Bir Bikram Shah Dev
(b) Sheikh Hasina Wajed
(c) King Jigme Singye Wangchuk
(d) Maumoon Abdul Gayoom

486 International Day of Older Persons was observed on
(a) September 27, 1999
(b) September 30, 1999
(c) October 11, 1999
(d) October 1, 1999

487 Mr. Graham Stewart Steins was in the news for which of the following reasons?
(a) He is the number of 2 men commission probing the January 22 incident of attack on Christians in Orissa
(b) He was an Australian missionary who was killed along with

his two sons in Manoharpur in Orissa

(c) An Australian missionary was beaten up & sent back to Australia

(d) None of the above

488 44th national Shooting Championship was held in November 2000 at

(a) Hyderabad
(b) Phillaur
(c) Nagpur
(d) Faridabad

489 The controversial book 'Vanity Incarnate', which is reported to have remarked about the tenth Sikh Guru, Sri Gobind Singh is written by

(a) Joginder Singh
(b) Hasrnam singh
(c) Harinder Singh
(d) Harjit Singh

490 Excluding an additional allocation of Rs. 22,900 crore for Prime Minister's Special Action Plan, the Union Cabinet approved the budgetory allocation for Ninth Five year Plan. It is approximately (in crores of Rs.)

(a) Rs. 37,400
(b) Rs. 4,74,000
(c) Rs. 3,74,000
(d) Rs. 47,400

491 The Hindi Pop album, 'O Meri Munni', scaling the charts and is approaching to be the first super-duper hit of 1999 was composed by whom among the following?

(a) Lucky Ali
(b) Daler Mehndi
(c) Ila Arun
(d) Remo Fernandes

492 The most important event of the Jagannath temple is the Rath Yatra where three 'Raths' or chariots are pulled by devotees from Jagannath temple. To which place is the 'rath' pulled?

(a) Subhadra bari
(b) Gundicha bari

(c) Dakshin bari
(d) Siddhi bari

493 M. F. Hussain's new museum of art and cinema is located in which of the following cities?
(a) Nagpur
(b) Hyderabad
(c) Bangalore
(d) Chennai

494 International Custom's Day was observed on
(a) 24th January
(b) 25th January
(c) 26th January
(d) 29th January

495 Poulami Ghatak is associated with
(a) Chess
(b) Tennis
(c) Table Tennis
(d) Swimming

496 Amman Ali Bangash is associated with
(a) Sarod
(b) Tabla
(c) Painting
(d) Flute

497 'Diplomacy for the Next Century' is book written by
(a) K. Natwar Singh
(b) Pavan Verma
(c) J. N. Dixit
(d) Abba Eban

498 World Table Tennis Championship was held in which of the following cities during April-May 1999?
(a) London
(b) Belgrade
(c) Buenos Aires
(d) Rome

499 Who among the following won the 1999 Australian Open Women's Single Title?
(a) Amelie Mauresmo

(b) Martina Hingis
(c) Lindsay Davenport
(d) Anna Kounikova

500 Who was the captain of the first Pakistani team after Independence, to tour India?
(a) A. H. Kardar
(b) Majid Khan
(c) Zaheer Abbas
(d) Sadiq Khan

501 Who among the following is the chairman of the National Commission for the Minorities?
(a) Mr. K. Neminath
(b) Justice D. P. Wadhwa
(c) Justice Mohammed Shamim
(d) Mr. M. Ravindra

502 Government declared observance of the year 2000 as the National Year for
(a) Children
(b) Famine Affected Families
(c) Older Persons
(d) Minorities

503 30th International Film Festival of India was held at
(a) Hyderabad
(b) Bangalore
(c) New Delhi
(d) Calcutta

504 President K. R. Narayanan conferred two Bharat Ratna awards on January 30, 1999. Who were recipients?
(a) Ravi Shankar & Gopinath Bordoloi
(b) M. F. Hussain & Gopinath Bordoloi
(c) Ravi Shankar & Zakir Hussain
(d) Ravi Shankar & Amartya Sen

505 Who among the following is the present Chairman of the Chief of the Staff Committee?
(a) Air Chief Marshall A. Y. Tipnis
(b) General S. Padmanabhan
(c) Admiral Sushil Kumar

(d) President K. R. Narayanan

506 What was the name of the Committee appointed by the Security and Exchange Board of India for finalising guidelines for Collective investment Scheme (CIS)
(a) S. A. Dave Committee
(b) S. T. Khanna Committee
(c) P. J. Rao Committee
(d) A. K. Aggarwal Committee

507 Hopman Cup is associated with which of the following games/sports?
(a) Football
(b) Tennis
(c) Golf
(d) Shooting

508 During 1998, the country's highest civilian honour Bharat ratna was not awarded to whom among the following?
(a) M. S. Subulakshmi
(b) C. Subramanium
(c) Jayaprakash Narayan
(d) Biju Patanaik

509 Who among the following was selected as the European Footballer of the Year for 1998?
(a) Davar Suker (Croatia)
(b) Michael Owen (England)
(c) Zinedine Zidane (France)
(d) Gaberiel Batistuta (Italy)

510 Two Indian architects figured in the nominees list at the 7th Triennial Aga Khan Award for Architecture Ceremony (1998) at Granada, Spain. One was Himangshu H. Parikh for Indore's slum Networking and the other was
(a) Charles Correa
(b) Anita Desai
(c) Rathin Dutta
(d) Gurmeet Singh

511 The award for the most outstanding athlete of the 13th Asian Games was given to
(a) Koji Ito (Japan)

(b) Talal Mansoor (Qatar)
(c) Kim Soon-Hyung (South Korea)
(d) Shunji Karube (Japan)

512 India signed Free Trade Agreement setting up a Free Trade Area with which of the following countries?
(a) Bangladesh
(b) Nepal
(c) Sri Lanka
(d) Bhutan

513 Which one of the following European countries did not accept the Euro currency?
(a) Sweden
(b) Germany
(c) Portugal
(d) Austria

514 Who among the following is/was the first elected US President to be impeached?
(a) John Glenn
(b) Andrew Jackson
(c) Bill Clinton
(d) Abraham Lincoln

515 Abdurrahman Wahid is the
(a) Prime Minister of Indonesia
(b) Prime Minister of Malaysia
(c) President of Indonesia
(d) President of Syria

516 Who among the following is the Director of the film, 'Saving Private Ryan'?
(a) Jackie Chan
(b) Jet Li
(c) Shekhar Kapur
(d) Steven Speelberg

517 Dingko Singh was in the news for winning a gold at the 13th Asian Games, is associated with
(a) Athletics
(b) Boxing
(c) Shooting

(d) Golf

518 Which hit Indian film of 1998 featuring Amir Khan was based on the Marlon Brando starrer 'On the Water Front'?
(a) Amanat
(b) Ghulam
(c) Khamoshi
(d) Border

519 The novel 'Paanch Anganon Wala Ghar' has been selected for the prestigious Vyas Samman, 1998. Who among the following has written this novel?
(a) Govind Mishra
(b) Savitri Devi
(c) Vinod Mishra
(d) Radhanath Rath

520 'The Ghosts of vasu Master' is a book written by
(a) Kavery Nabisan
(b) Githa Hariharan
(c) Kandadai Seshadri
(d) Sanjay Subrahmanyam

521 Which one of the following Indian films has won all top awards, including a Golden Pyramid Award for the best film, at the 23rd Cairo International Film Festival?
(a) The Terrorist
(b) Jaha Tum Le Chalo
(c) Fire
(d) China Gate

522 At the 13th asian Games, which of the following women weightlifters set a new world record in the 48-kg category?
(a) Kay Thi Win (Myanmar)
(b) Sri Indriyani (Indonesia)
(c) Liu Xiuhua (China)
(d) Polsak Udomporn (Thailand)

523 Apart from Rosa Kutty and Jyotirmoyee Sikdar, who were other two members of the Indian women's 4 X 400 metres relay team, which won a silver medal at the Bangkok Asian Games?
(a) Jincy Philip and K. M. Beenamol
(b) Jincy Philip and P. T. Usha

(c) P. T. Usha and Sunita Rani
(d) K. M. Beenamol and Sunita Rani

524 Which Indian Athlete won the maximum number of gold medals at the 8th SAF Games held in Kathmandu in September-October, 1999?
(a) Sunita Rani
(b) Bula Chaudhary
(c) Rosa Kutty
(d) Nisha Millet

525 Who among the following was chosen as Miss Universe 1999?
(a) Ms. Veronique Caloc (France)
(b) Ms. Pick Lim Lin Teoh (Venezuela)
(c) Ms. Mpule Kwelagobe (Botswana)
(d) Ms. Annie Thomas (India)

526 The 1998 Dada Saheb Phalke award was given to
(a) B. R. Chopra
(b) Dilip Kumar
(c) Shekhar Kapur
(d) Shyam Benegal

527 Ms. Arundhati Roy, who led a march "Rally for the Valley", is the author of the 1998 Booker Prize winning book named
(a) The God of Small Things
(b) Worshipping False Gods
(c) Equal Music
(d) A Suitable Boy

528 Which of the following companies has become the first private Internet Service Provider (ISP) to start Internet Services in India?
(a) Samtech International Ltd.
(b) Satyam Online Ltd.
(c) Cybermate & Srivel Ltd.
(d) H. P. Infrastructure Corporation Ltd.

529 Ritwik Bhattacharya is associated with which of the following games/sports?
(a) Squash
(b) Chess
(c) Table Tennis
(d) Hockey

530 Mr. Manohar Parrikar was in the news for which of the following reasons?
(a) He became Chief Minister of Goa
(b) He was appointed as governor of Goa
(c) he became the Chief Minister of Mizoram
(d) None of the above

531 Who among the following has painted the largest silk scroll painting in the world, containing the pictures of Hindu deities and has an entry in the 'Guinness Book of World Records'?
(a) Sujit Kumar Chatterjee
(b) Ranjit Bharuch
(c) Sanat Kumar Chatterjee
(d) Shefali Gulati

532 Who among the following is the present Solicitor-General of India?
(a) Mr. C. S. Vaidyanathan
(b) Mr. Soli Sorabjee
(c) Mr. R. M. Vijayanunni
(d) Mr. Harish Salve

533 'Stone Raft' and 'It's Always Possible' are the two books written respectively by
(a) Jose Saramago & Kiran Bedi
(b) Ian McEwan & Kiran Bedi
(c) Vikram Seth & Som Anand
(d) Ben Hecht & Mohd. Azharuddin

534 What is the name of the Dhaka's district and session judge, who was in the news for delivering the historic judgement of passing death sentence against 15 of the 19 accused, in the case of killing Bangladesh's founding leader late Sheikh Mujibur Rehman, on August 15, 1975?
(a) Kazi Golam Rasul
(b) Abdellatif Filali
(c) Saeed Al Abdullah
(d) None of these

535 Kanishka World Cup for Blind held in India was won by
(a) South Africa
(b) Pakistan
(c) India

(d) Sri Lanka

536 The 1998 India International Trade fair (Asia's largest International Trade Fair) was held during November 2000 at

(a) Calcutta
(b) Mumbai
(c) new Delhi
(d) Chennai

537 Who among the following was given the 1998 United States Professional Tennis Registry Pro of the Year Award (for India)?

(a) Zeeshan Ali
(b) Akhtar Ali
(c) Tejbir Bhandari
(d) Premjit Lal

538 Who among the following received the 1998-99 prestigious Rajiv Gandhi Khel Ratna Award?

(a) Jyotirmoyee Sikdar
(b) Shiny Wilson
(c) Santosh Yadav
(d) Kunjarani devi

539 World AIDS day was observed recently on

(a) November 30
(b) December 1
(c) December 3
(d) December 10

540 The abbreviation 'NHRDF' stands for

(a) National Human Resource Development
(b) National Horticulture Research and Development Foundation
(c) National Highway Research and Development Foundation
(d) National Hydro-Electric Research and Development Federation

541 In which of the following countries, during November 1998, more then 7000 people were killed in a hurricane?

(a) Guatemala and Honduras
(b) Costa Rica and Nicaragua
(c) Honduras and Nicaragua
(d) Costa Rica and Honduras

542 10th International Congress on Immunology was held at

(a) Calcutta
(b) Chennai
(c) Bangalore
(d) New Delhi

543 The final of the Durand Cup Football tournament held at New Delhi in November 2000 was won by
(a) Mahindra & Mahindra
(b) Air India
(c) East Bengal
(d) Mohun Bagan

544 Which of the following committees was set up to report on anomalies and disparities in pay and allowances
(a) Ajit Kumar Committee
(b) Prabhat Kumar Committee
(c) Ashok Kumar Committee
(d) Gangopadhyay Committee

545 Bardoloi Trophy is associated with which of the following games/ sports?
(a) Football
(b) Hockey
(c) Basketball
(d) Table Tennis

546 Nirad C. Chaudhuri who died during 1999 at the age of 101 years was a famous
(a) Musician
(b) Novelist
(c) Painter
(d) Athlete

547 Under which Article of the Constitution, the President of India appoints judges of the High Court after consultation with the Chief Justice of India
(a) Article 215 (1)
(b) Article 216 (1)
(c) Article 217 (1)
(d) Article 222 (1)

548 Who among the following at the age of 77 years has become the world's oldest space traveller (coincidentally he was also the first

American in Orbit on February 20, 1962)?
(a) Brian Watson
(b) John Glenn
(c) Javier Solana
(d) Paul Reeves

549 Who among the following won 1999 Booker Prize for his novel 'Disgrace'?
(a) Anita Desai
(b) Namita Gokhale
(c) J. M. Coetzee
(d) Salman Rushdie

550 International day for Eradication of Poverty was observed on
(a) October 14
(b) October 15
(c) October 16
(d) October 17

551 Who among the following won the 1999 Nobel Peace Prize?
(a) Medicines Sans Frontieres (Doctors without Medicine)
(b) Robert C. Laughlin and Daniel C. Tsui
(c) Robert Furchgott and David Trimble
(d) John Hume and Louis Ignarro

552 Rashtriya Sankalpa Diwas is observed in India on the death anniversary of
(a) Chaudhary Charan Singh
(b) Indira Gandhi
(c) Jawahar Lal Nehru
(d) Sanjay Gandhi

553 The book 'The Story of My Childhood and Boyhead' is written by
(a) Dr. Satish Goel
(b) P. N. Haksar
(c) Dr. A. R. Kidwai
(d) Vikram Seth

554 Madame Tussaud's Museum, which was in the news is famous for its
(a) Stone Sculptures
(b) Wooden figures
(c) Wax figures

(d) Collection of Vintage Cars

555 Which of the following is the specially designed scheme for the welfare of the Indian women, introduced recently by the General Insurance?

(a) Rajeswari
(b) Bhagya Rajeshwari
(c) Bhagyashree
(d) None of these

556 Dr. B. C. Roy National Award for Eminent Doctor was given in June 2000 to

(a) Dr. Hari Gautam
(b) Dr. D. P. Bakshi
(c) Dr. Jagnnath Pathak
(d) Dr. R. K. Paril

557 The world's longest under-water natural gas pipeline stretching 850 km connects which of the following two countries?

(a) Norway-Britain
(b) Norway-France
(c) Norway-Germany
(d) Finland-Germany

558 Which one of the following prestigious prize has been awarded to the Ramakrishna Mission, for its pioneering role in economic and political transformation through non-violence?

(a) 1998 Jawaharlal Nehru Award
(b) 1998 Getz World Peace Prize
(c) 1998 Nobel Peace Prize
(d) 1998 Gandhi Peace Prize

559 'Worshipping False Gods' is a book written by

(a) Arun Shourie
(b) R. K. Narayan
(c) Harbans Singh
(d) Salman Rushdie

560 Florence Griffith Joyner, who revolutionised the women's athletics scene died at the age of 38. She was holding the world record for

(a) 100 m & 200 m race
(b) 100 m & 400 m race
(c) 200 m & 400 m race

(d) 400 m & 110 m hurdles

561 Who among the following political leaders has coined the term "PE-Y2K" (the Political Economic year 2000-Problem)
(a) Gerhard Schroeder
(b) Bill Clinton
(c) Atal Bihari Vajpayee
(d) Boris Yeltsin

562 What was the theme of the 1998 World Hobitat Day observed on October 5?
(a) Safer Cities
(b) Safer Skies
(c) Safer Oceans
(d) Safer Drinking Water

563 The first World Cup Cricket Tournament for the blind was played in which of the following cities in November 1998?
(a) New Delhi
(b) Bangalore
(c) Kanpur
(d) Calcutta

564 Which of the following Indian feature films directed by Nobyendu Chatterjee won the special prize of the festival organising committee at the Sixth Pyongyang International Film Festival held in September 1998 in North Korea?
(a) Sauda
(b) Mrityudand
(c) Karm
(d) None of these

565 Who among the following was the first U.S. President to resign from office?
(a) Ronald Reagon
(b) Richard Nixon
(c) James Polk
(d) John Tyler

566 Roopa Unnikrishnan, who won the gold medal for India at the 16th Commonwealth Games held at Kuala Lumpur, is associated with which of the following games/sports?
(a) Shooting

(b) Badminton
(c) Table Tennis
(d) Athletics

567 The prestigious 900 MW-Boghliar hydro-electric project is being set up on which of the following rivers and will be meeting the energy requirements of which state?
(a) Chenab, Punjab
(b) Beas, J & K
(c) Chenab, J & K
(d) Ghagghar, Punjab

568 Which of the following cities was the venue of the 12th NAM summit held in September, 1998?
(a) Durban
(b) Colombo
(c) Lusaka
(d) Belgrade

569 Shubha Mudgal is a noted
(a) Hindustani Classical Vocalist
(b) Painter
(c) Kathak dancer
(d) Cartoonist

570 13th Asian Games Football Championship was held in December 1998 at
(a) Tokyo
(b) Bangkok
(c) Kuala Lumpur
(d) Taipei

571 Who is the first woman to become the President of the International Parliamentary Union (IPU)?
(a) Rita Verma
(b) Najma Heptullah
(c) Mohsina Kidwai
(d) Sushma Swaraj

572 Akira Kurasova, who died in 1998, was a celebrated film maker from
(a) Russia
(b) South Korea

(c) Japan
(d) China

573 Who among the following were selected for the H.K. Firodia Awards for Excellence in Science and Technology for the year 2000?
(a) Dr. R. A. Mashelkar and dr. D. D. Bhawalkar
(b) Dr. R. Chidambaram and Prof. Claude Cohen
(c) Prof. K. Kasturirangan and Shri S. K. Sikka
(d) Dr. A. P. J. Abdul Kalam and Dr. R. Chidambaram

574 The abbreviation GMPCS stands for
(a) Global Mobile Personal Communication
(b) Global Maritime Project for Communication through Satellite
(c) Global Mobile Personal Communication by satellite
(d) Global Mobile Project for Communication by Satellite

575 What is the name of the fourteen seater multi-role, indigenous aircraft being designed by the national Aerospace Laboratories which is scheduled to have its first flight before the end of 1999?
(a) Saras
(b) Akshay
(c) Ambar
(d) Hans

576 The United nations Organisation completed how many years of its existence by the end of 2000?
(a) 50
(b) 45
(c) 54
(d) 55

577 Which of the following is envisaged in Hybrid Mail Service introduced by the Department of Posts and Telegraphs?
(a) A message manually brought to the post office can be sent electonically to another post office for delivery at the premises of the customer through postman
(b) A message submitted at a rural post office can be relayed on phone to another post office in a neighbouring State
(c) A message submitted at any post office can be transmitted to a ship on sea
(d) A message brought to the post office on a floppy diskette can be sent manually to another post office.

578 Which of the following is the function of National Committee on Children?
(a) It will monitor the welfare scheme of children
(b) It will control the use of child labour in factories
(c) It will review the developmental programmes implemented by various State governments for children
(d) It will review and analyse the situation of children in India

579 In which of the following groups of States, the Government of India launched the World Bank assisted IX India Population Project
(a) Assam, Tripura, Bihar
(b) Assam, West Bengal, Rajasthan
(c) Assam, Karnataka, Rajasthan
(d) Assam, Andhra Pradesh, Karnataka

580 Koneru Hampy is associated with which of the following games/ sports
(a) Athletics
(b) Chess
(c) Golf
(d) Hockey

Answers

1	(c)	2	(a)	3	(b)	4	(c)	5	(d)
6	(d)	7	(a)	8	(b)	9	(d)	10	(a)
11	(b)	12	(c)	13	(a)	14	(d)	15	(a)
16	(a)	17	(c)	18	(b)	19	(b)	20	(a)
21	(b)	22	(c)	23	(b)	24	(c)	25	(c)
26	(a)	27	(b)	28	(a)	29	(b)	30	(a)
31	(b)	32	(d)	33	(d)	34	(c)	35	(b)
36	(c)	37	(a)	38	(a)	39	(a)	40	(c)
41	(b)	42	(a)	43	(b)	44	(b)	45	(a)
46	(c)	47	(b)	48	(a)	49	(a)	50	(a)
51	(c)	52	(b)	53	(b)	54	(a)	55	(d)
56	(b)	57	(a)	58	(d)	59	(c)	60	(a)
61	(b)	62	(c)	63	(c)	64	(b)	65	(b)
66	(d)	67	(c)	68	(b)	69	(a)	70	(b)
71	(a)	72	(b)	73	(c)	74	(d)	75	(a)
76	(b)	77	(a)	78	(d)	79	(c)	80	(b)
81	(c)	82	(c)	83	(b)	84	(c)	85	(b)
86	(c)	87	(a)	88	(b)	89	(c)	90	(b)
91	(b)	92	(d)	93	(a)	94	(a)	95	(c)
96	(d)	97	(b)	98	(c)	99	(b)	100	(a)
101	(b)	102	(c)	103	(d)	104	(d)	105	(b)
106	(a)	107	(b)	108	(c)	109	(c)	110	(b)
111	(b)	112	(c)	113	(c)	114	(c)	115	(d)
116	(d)	117	(b)	118	(a)	119	(b)	120	(b)
121	(b)	122	(c)	123	(b)	124	(b)	125	(a)
126	(c)	127	(a)	128	(d)	129	(d)	130	(b)
131	(c)	132	(d)	133	(c)	134	(c)	135	(b)
136	(b)	137	(a)	138	(c)	139	(c)	140	(d)
141	(c)	142	(b)	143	(c)	144	(d)	145	(a)
146	(c)	147	(b)	148	(d)	149	(a)	150	(a)

151	(a)	152	(a)	153	(b)	154	(b)	155	(d)
156	(d)	157	(a)	158	(b)	159	(b)	160	(b)
161	(b)	162	(d)	163	(c)	164	(a)	165	(c)
166	(b)	167	(a)	168	(b)	169	(a)	170	(d)
171	(a)	172	(a)	173	(c)	174	(a)	175	(a)
176	(c)	177	(a)	178	(b)	179	(c)	180	(c)
181	(d)	182	(c)	183	(b)	184	(a)	185	(d)
186	(b)	187	(c)	188	(b)	189	(b)	190	(b)
191	(a)	192	(b)	193	(a)	194	(b)	195	(c)
196	(d)	197	(a)	198	(a)	199	(a)	200	(d)
201	(b)	202	(b)	203	(a)	204	(c)	205	(b)
206	(d)	207	(c)	208	(c)	209	(b)	210	(a)
211	(c)	212	(a)	213	(a)	214	(b)	215	(a)
216	(b)	217	(a)	218	(c)	219	(c)	220	(d)
221	(c)	222	(a)	223	(c)	224	(b)	225	(c)
226	(b)	227	(c)	228	(a)	229	(b)	230	(b)
231	(c)	232	(a)	233	(c)	234	(c)	235	(c)
236	(c)	237	(b)	238	(d)	239	(d)	240	(c)
241	(d)	242	(a)	243	(a)	244	(d)	245	(b)
246	(c)	247	(a)	248	(b)	249	(a)	250	(a)
251	(c)	252	(a)	253	(b)	254	(b)	255	(c)
256	(c)	257	(c)	258	(a)	259	(d)	260	(c)
261	(a)	262	(c)	263	(a)	264	(c)	265	(b)
266	(d)	267	(a)	268	(a)	269	(b)	270	(c)
271	(b)	272	(b)	273	(a)	274	(b)	275	(d)
276	(a)	277	(a)	278	(c)	279	(a)	280	(d)
281	(a)	282	(c)	283	(c)	284	(c)	285	(c)
286	(d)	287	(a)	288	(a)	289	(b)	290	(a)
291	(d)	292	(b)	293	(a)	294	(c)	295	(a)
296	(b)	297	(d)	298	(a)	299	(d)	300	(b)
301	(c)	302	(b)	303	(c)	304	(a)	305	(a)
306	(b)	307	(c)	308	(c)	309	(c)	310	(a)

311 (b) 312 (c) 313 (d) 314 (a) 315 (a)
316 (a) 317 (b) 318 (c) 319 (d) 320 (d)
321 (b) 322 (a) 323 (d) 324 (a) 325 (a)
326 (a) 327 (a) 328 (d) 329 (c) 330 (a)
331 (b) 332 (b) 333 (b) 334 (b) 335 (c)
336 (a) 337 (a) 338 (c) 339 (a) 340 (b)
341 (b) 342 (c) 343 (c) 344 (b) 345 (d)
346 (c) 347 (b) 348 (a) 349 (a) 350 (b)
351 (a) 352 (a) 353 (d) 354 (b) 355 (b)
356 (a) 357 (c) 358 (a) 359 (a) 360 (c)
361 (b) 362 (a) 363 (a) 364 (a) 365 (b)
366 (d) 367 (b) 368 (c) 379 (b) 370 (b)
371 (a) 372 (a) 373 (d) 374 (a) 375 (a)
376 (b) 377 (c) 378 (c) 379 (a) 380 (c)
381 (b) 382 (a) 383 (b) 384 (b) 385 (d)
386 (c) 387 (b) 388 (a) 389 (a) 390 (b)
391 (d) 392 (a) 393 (b) 394 (c) 395 (c)
396 (a) 397 (a) 398 (b) 399 (a) 400 (c)
401 (c) 402 (b) 403 (a) 404 (a) 405 (c)
406 (c) 407 (b) 408 (c) 409 (b) 410 (c)
411 (b) 412 (a) 413 (b) 414 (b) 415 (a)
416 (a) 417 (b) 418 (d) 419 (a) 420 (b)
421 (b) 422 (a) 423 (a) 424 (a) 425 (b)
426 (b) 427 (a) 428 (b) 429 (b) 430 (a)
431 (b) 432 (a) 433 (a) 434 (c) 435 (c)
436 (b) 437 (b) 438 (a) 439 (d) 440 (a)
441 (d) 442 (d) 443 (a) 444 (c) 445 (a)
446 (b) 447 (a) 448 (b) 449 (b) 450 (a)
451 (b) 452 (b) 453 (c) 454 (b) 455 (c)
456 (c) 457 (a) 458 (a) 459 (b) 460 (a)
461 (b) 462 (c) 463 (a) 464 (a) 465 (d)
466 (b) 467 (d) 468 (a) 469 (a) 470 (d)

471	(b)	472	(b)	473	(c)	474	(a)	475	(d)
476	(b)	477	(a)	478	(c)	479	(a)	480	(b)
481	(d)	482	(d)	483	(a)	484	(c)	485	(a)
486	(d)	487	(b)	488	(b)	489	(c)	490	(c)
491	(d)	492	(b)	493	(b)	494	(c)	495	(c)
496	(a)	497	(d)	498	(b)	499	(b)	500	(a)
501	(c)	502	(c)	503	(a)	504	(a)	505	(c)
506	(a)	507	(b)	508	(d)	509	(c)	510	(a)
511	(a)	512	(c)	513	(a)	514	(c)	515	(c)
516	(d)	517	(b)	518	(b)	519	(a)	520	(b)
521	(a)	522	(c)	523	(a)	524	(d)	525	(c)
526	(a)	527	(a)	528	(b)	529	(a)	530	(a)
531	(c)	532	(d)	533	(a)	534	(a)	535	(a)
536	(c)	537	(b)	538	(a)	539	(b)	540	(b)
541	(c)	542	(d)	543	(d)	544	(a)	545	(a)
546	(b)	547	(c)	548	(b)	549	(c)	550	(c)
551	(a)	552	(b)	553	(b)	554	(c)	555	(c)
556	(a)	557	(b)	558	(d)	559	(a)	560	(a)
561	(c)	562	(a)	563	(a)	564	(a)	565	(b)
566	(a)	567	(c)	568	(a)	569	(a)	570	(b)
571	(b)	572	(c)	573	(a)	574	(c)	575	(a)
576	(d)	577	(a)	578	(d)	579	(c)	580	(b)

IT BASIC

1. A computer consists of
   (a) A Central Processing Unit
   (b) A Memory Unit
   (c) Input and Output Units
   (d) All of the above

2. Which of the following memories is capable of operating at electronic speed?
   (a) Semiconductor memory
   (b) Magnetic disks
   (c) Magnetic drums
   (d) Magnetic Tapes

3. Which of the following is the fastest?
   (a) CPU
   (b) Sensors, mechanical controllers
   (c) Vide terminals
   (d) Magnetic disks and tapes

4. A collections of wires connects several devices is called
   (a) Link
   (b) Bus
   (c) Cables
   (d) Bidirectional wires

5. Storage device used to compensate the differences in flow of data is known as
   (a) Main storage
   (b) Auxiliary storage
   (c) Buffer
   (d) Core memory

6. Microprocessors can be used to make
   (a) Computers
   (b) Calculators
   (c) Digital systems
   (d) All of the above

7. The time elapsed between the initiation of memory operation and the completion of that operation is known as
   (a) Memory Cycle

(b) Skip time
(c) Memory access time
(d) Transfer access time

8. Which memory is volatile?
(a) RAM
(b) ROM
(c) PROM
(d) EPROM

9. Which of the following memories has the shortest access time?
(a) Cache memory
(b) Magnetic bubble memory
(c) Magnetic core memory
(d) RAM

10. Which of the following produces the best quality graphics reproduction?
(a) Laser Printer
(b) Ink Jet Printer
(c) Plotter
(d) Dot Matrix Printer

11. The operating system manages
(a) Memory
(b) Processor
(c) Disk and I/O devices
(d) All of the above

12. Moving process from main memory to disk is called
(a) Scheduling
(b) Caching
(c) Swapping
(d) Spooling

13. Sending a file from your PC's memory or disk to another computer is called
(a) Downloading
(b) Logging on
(c) Uploading
(d) Tracing on

14. The process of copying data from a memory location is called
(a) Heading

(b) Writing
(c) Controlling
(d) Hand-shaking

15. Which of the following computer is the least powerful?
(a) Mini Computer
(b) Micro Computer
(c) Mainframe Computer
(d) Super Computer

16. Which of the following memories is an optical memory?
(a) CD Rom
(b) Floppy Disk
(c) Bubble Memory
(d) Care memory

17. Computer instructions in a program are performed in what order?
(a) Random
(b) Consecutive
(c) Parallel
(d) Any of the abone

18. Unlike detail..................... do not supply detailed description of modules but graphically describe a system data and how the data interacts with the system?
(a) Program BFO
(b) Program Graphics
(c) Flow chart DED
(d) Structure, DFD

19. Quality information is measured by
(a) Validity
(b) Polymorphism Accuracy
(c) Precision
(d) All of the above

20. Unprocessed facts and figure are .... where as processed facts and figures are ....
(a) Information, data
(b) Data, information
(c) Tables, relationship
(d) Files, reports

21. Following activities can be performed if one has an access to the INTERNET
    (a) You can refer to the picture of an art gallery.
    (b) You can have electronic copy of journals and magazine from the INTERNET
    (c) You can send mail accross the boundaries in no time
    (d) All of the above

22. Host and local networks in Internet are grouped together into
    (a) Domains
    (b) Servers
    (c) Hosts
    (d) None of the above

23. The full form of SLIP is
    (a) Serial Low but Intellectual Protocol
    (b) Serial Line Internet Protocal
    (c) Serial Line Interconnected Protocaol
    (d) None of the above

24. The protocaol that is used to transfer files from one machine to another on Internet is
    (a) TCP/IP
    (b) PTP
    (c) HTTP
    (d) PPP

25. Any file, which can incorporate sound, pictures, text, graphics togather may be called
    (a) Hypertext document
    (b) Text file
    (c) Compiler
    (d) Interpreter

26. The following language is an Object Oriented Programing language
    (a) Java
    (b) C
    (c) Pascal
    (d) None of the above

27. A client server system can contain only
    (a) One server
    (b) Two servers

(c) Three servers
(d) Any number of servers

28. The diagram, which indicates data flow, is
(a) Flow chart
(b) Structured chart
(c) All of the above
(d) None of the above

29. Who governs the Internet
(a) ISOC
(b) IAB
(c) AETF
(d) All of the above

30. Theory of information was proposed by
(a) Daniel Bell
(b) Wersing
(c) Nenling
(d) Shannon / Wearer

31. ________ are the programs that claim to do something but do something completely different and damage the computer.
(a) Virus
(b) Worm
(c) Trojens
(d) Either 2 or 3

32. What is the name of the computer based EMMS that provides a command from where users can check in at their convenience, post message, actively exchange ideas and participate in ongoing discussion.
(a) E-mail
(b) Bulletin Board System (BBS)
(c) Teleconferencing
(d) Video Conferencing

33. A system bus connects
(a) CPU, Memory, I/O components
(b) CPU, Hard disk, Memory
(c) Memory, I/O components
(d) None of the above

34. Which of the following views attacks the executable files?

(a) Friday the 13th
(b) Lenigh Virus
(c) Scores Virus
(d) All of the above

35. Pick out the kind of storage device, which can be used around
(a) Hard disk
(b) System cabinet
(c) Diskette
(d) Main memory

36. RAM in a computer stands for
(a) Read to Access Memory
(b) Read At-a-time Memory
(c) Reading Available Memory
(d) Random Access Memory

37. A factor which would strongly influence a business person to adopt a computer is its
(a) Accuracy
(b) Reliability
(c) Speed
(d) All of the above

38. Which of the following is not an advantage of erasable optical disk?
(a) The capacity of an erasable disk is very high in comparison to magnetic disk.
(b) The erasable optical disk are portable
(c) The erasable optical disks are highly reliable but have a short life.
(d) Erasable optical disk also uses format that makes semi-random access feasible.

39. Which of the following term is wrongly named?
(a) PSTN Public Switched Telephone Network
(b) ISDN Integrated Services Digital Network
(c) PSDN Public Switched data Network
(d) None of the above

40. A good Graphics editor can
(a) Enlarge a diagram
(b) Rotate a diagram
(c) Move a diagram

(d) All of the above

41. Principle of ensuring security and recovery in case of breach of security is
    (a) To minimize damage
    (b) Recovery
    (c) Present's detect
    (d) All of the above

42. The retrieval of information from the computer is defined as
    (a) Collection of data
    (b) Data retrieval operations
    (c) Output
    (d) Data output collection

43. Which of the following is the most powerful type of computer
    (a) Minicomputer
    (b) Super computer
    (c) Micro computer
    (d) Super conductor

44. The most common input device used today is the
    (a) Motherboard
    (b) Central Processing Unit
    (c) Key board
    (d) System Unit

45. For protecting floppy disks and the software those contain, they should not be
    (a) Bent
    (b) Brought near Magnets
    (c) Exposed to Sun or heat
    (d) All of the above

46. Processor of all computers whether micro, mini or main frame, miust have
    (a) Primary Storage
    (b) ALU
    (c) Control Unit
    (d) All of the above

47. What kind of hardware was used by first generation computers?
    (a) Transistors
    (b) Valves

(c) ICs
(d) SSI

48. ROM is composed of
(a) Magnetic Cores
(b) Microprocessor
(c) Photoelectric Cells
(d) Floppy Disks

49. The first mechanical computer designed by Charles Babbage was called
(a) Analytical Engine
(b) Abacus
(c) Calculator
(d) Processor

50. A Communication device that combines transmission from several I/O device into line is a
(a) Connector
(b) Modifier
(c) Multiplexer
(d) Full duplex line

51. Which of the following items is not used in Local Area Networks (LAN)?
(a) Computer
(b) Modem
(c) Printer
(d) cable

52. Different Computers are connected to LAN by a Cable and
(a) Modem
(b) Interface Card
(c) Special Wires
(d) Telephone Lines

53. Messages from one computer terminal can be sent to another by using data networks. The message to be sent is converted to an electronic digital signal, transmitted via a cable, telephone or satellite and then converted back again at the receiving end. What is this system of sending message called?
(a) Paperless Office
(b) Electronic Mail

(c) Global Network
(d) Electronic Newspaper

54. Which data communication method is used for sending data in both directions at the same time?
(a) Super Duplex
(b) Simplex
(c) Half Duplex
(d) Full Duplex

55. Computer virus can multiply and spread from one Computer to another by means of
(a) Injected disks
(b) Links to a network
(c) Download program from a bulletien board
(d) All of the above

56. Which of the following is the most commonly experienced symptom of a computer virus attack?
(a) System memory is increased
(b) Available disk space is increased
(c) Program loading takes longer than normal
(d) Disk access time is reduced

57. Since virus are only a form of software, they primarily infect
(a) Data
(b) Programs
(c) Hardware
(d) Peripherals

58. What is the name of the program, which claims to be something useful but is indentation programmed to be malicious?
(a) Double Action Virus
(b) Trojan Horse
(c) Logic Bomb
(d) Time Bomb

59. A hard disk becomes totally inaccessible, when a computer virus corrupts its
(a) Partition table
(b) File allocation table
(c) Route directory
(d) Boot sector

60. A computer program consists of
(a) A computer flow chart
(b) Algorithms
(c) Algorithms written in computer language
(d) Discrete logical steps.

61. In computer terminology, a compiler is
(a) A person who computes source programs
(b) The same thing as a programmer
(c) Key-punch operator
(d) A program, which translates a source program into object code.

62. Control unit is often called the ________ of a digital computer
(a) Nerve centre
(b) Master dispatcher
(c) Clock
(d) All of the above

63. Which one of the following is not a key feture of Von Neumann Archticture Machine?
(a) A CPU which includes an ALU and CU.
(b) A main memory system
(c) An Input / Output system
(d) Double path between the main memory and control unit

64. The method in which processing of data is done by using more than one CPU is called
(a) Multiprogramming
(b) Multiprocessing
(c) Both (a) & (b)
(d) Batch processing

65. Pick one of the following, which is an essential component of system software and consists of procedure for managing computer resources
(a) Compiler
(b) Operating system
(c) Assembler
(d) Loader

66. In the context of a small business office, a heavy duty laser printer can be connected directly to the LAN via an optional NIC, the full form of which is

(a) National Information Centre
(b) Network Interface Card
(c) New Information Collection
(d) None of the above

67. An inventory management system should answer the questions
(a) What and why
(b) When and how much
(c) Where and when
(d) Who and why

68. Quantitative techniques used to solve business problems are called
(a) Operations science
(b) Operations management
(c) Operations research
(d) Management operations

69. The minimum requirement of Multimedia processor should be
(a) 286
(b) 386
(c) 486
(d) Pentium

70. A signal processor is always embedded in __________ to provide additional capabilities without affecting the CPU
(a) MIDI
(b) Sound Card
(c) Microphone
(d) WAV file

71. The file format for a Music only file is
(a) VOC
(b) RIFF
(c) WAV
(d) MIDI

72. Which of the following does not effect the quality of video playing on the computer?
(a) Frame Rate (Fps)
(b) Speed of Action
(c) Size of Video
(d) Number of colors

73. The bill of materials is a document

(a) Containing information about a detailed list of goods
(b) Containing a detatiled list of the product structure required to manufature a finished product
(c) Used for forecasting of product sales
(d) None of the above

74. Commonly used backup storage in office are
(a) Floppy disks
(b) Cartridge takes
(c) Compact disks
(d) All of the above.

75. __________ is organized by events and activities
(a) Bar Chart
(b) Gantt Chart
(c) Pert Chart
(d) Pie Chart

76. Which of the following is the default document view in MS-WORD application?
(a) Normal view
(b) Page layout view
(c) Outline view
(d) None of the above

77. To quit MS-DOS prompt and return to windows, type
(a) Quit
(b) Exit
(c) Double Click
(d) Single Click

78. MIDI stands for
(a) Musical Instuments Digital Interface
(b) Multimedia interface driver installation
(c) Multimedia Installation with Digitized Interaction
(d) None of the above

79. API means
(a) Application Programme Interface
(b) Application Production Industry
(c) Application Program for instructors
(d) None of the above

80. DLL stands for

(a) .Database Link Library
(b) Dynamic Link Library
(c) Data Link Library
(d) None of the above

81. DDE stands for
(a) Dynamic Data Exchange
(b) Dynamic Database Engine
(c) Dyanamic data Extension
(d) None of the above

82. A graphic representation of an information system is called
(a) Flow chart
(b) Data flow chart
(c) Pictogram
(d) dvn chart

83. A statement by statement description of a procedure is detailed in a
(a) Written narrative
(b) Procedural log
(c) Record Layout
(d) System flow chart

84. Data base preparation would be most difficult in a
(a) Supermarket
(b) Bank
(c) Hospital
(d) College or university

85. MRP stands for
(a) Management Resource Planning
(b) Market Research Planning
(c) Manufacturing Planning
(d) Material Requirement Planning

86. Sales invoicing is a
(a) Pre-sales activity
(b) Job of finance department
(c) Post sales activity
(d) All of the above

87. A system must be composed of more than one
(a) Subsystem
(b) Elements

(c) Supersystem
(d) All of the above

88. Sales figure in the market forecast file are updated by the
(a) Sales analysis procedures
(b) Sales forecasting procedures
(c) Market Research Procedures
(d) All of the above

89. To make a group active
(a) Minimize a Window
(b) Open a group Window
(c) Maximize a Window
(d) Restore a Window

90. Which of the following is used as secondary storage
(a) CPU
(b) Memory
(c) I/O unit
(d) Disks

91. Which of the following is the fastest
(a) CPU
(b) Magnetic Disk
(c) Video terminals
(d) Sensor and Mechanical Controllers

92. A 32 bit microprocessor has the word length equal to
(a) 2 bytes
(b) 1 bytes
(c) 8 bytes
(d) 4 bytes

93. A dumb terminal has
(a) An embedded microprocessor
(b) Extensive Memory
(c) Independent Processing Capacity
(d) A Keyboard and a Screen

94. The primary purpose of an operating system is to
(a) Make a computer easier to use
(b) Keep system programmes busy
(c) Make the most efficient use of hardware
(d) Allow people to use the computers

95. The heart of any computer is the
    (a) CPU
    (b) Memory
    (c) I/O unit
    (d) Disks

96. The time clapsed between the invitation of a memory operations and the competetors of operation is known as
    (a) Memory cycle time
    (b) Memory access time
    (c) Transfer time
    (d) Skip time

97. Which memory is volatile
    (a) ROM
    (b) EPROM
    (c) RAM
    (d) PROM

98. Which of the following memories has the shortest access time?
    (a) Magnetic bubble memory
    (b) Cache Memory
    (c) Magnetic Core Memory
    (d) RAM

99. Daisy wheel printer is a type of
    (a) Impact printer
    (b) Matrix printer
    (c) Laser printer
    (d) Manual printer

100. A device or peripheral equipment which is not in direct communication with CPU of a computer is known as
    (a) Online device
    (b) Channel
    (c) Off-line device
    (d) Intelligent terminal

101. Special software to create a job queue is called a/an
    (a) TOS
    (b) Interpreter
    (c) Spooler
    (d) Linkage editor

102. Which of the following performs modulation and demodulation?
    (a) Fibre optic
    (b) Satellite
    (c) Modem
    (d) Waxial cable

103. Devices on one network can communicate with devices on another network via a
    (a) File server
    (b) Utility server
    (c) Printer server
    (d) Gateway

104. A device that can convert digital signal to analog signal is
    (a) A packet
    (b) An emulator
    (c) A modem
    (d) A code

105. Demodulation is the process of
    (a) Converting digital signals to analog signal
    (b) Converting analog signals to digital signals.
    (c) Combining may high speed channels into one high speed channel
    (d) Dividing the high speed signals into frequency bands

106. The communication mode that support data in both directions at the same time is
    (a) Duplex
    (b) Simplex
    (c) Half-Duplex
    (d) Multiplex

107. One of the main features that distinguishes microprocessor from microcomputers is
    (a) Words are usually larger in microprocessor
    (b) Words are shorter in microprocessors
    (c) Microprocessors do not contain I/O devices
    (d) Computers are not fully integrated

108. The input unit of a computer
    (a) Feeds data to the CPU or memory
    (b) Retrives data from CPU

(c) Retrives data from memory
(d) Directs all units'

109. A collection of wires that connects several devices is called
(a) Link
(b) Bidirkctional wires
(c) Cables
(d) Bus

110 Modern computers compared to earlier computers are
(a) Faster and larger
(b) Less reliable
(c) Large and stronger
(d) Faster and smaller

111. Integrated circuits were used in the following generation of computers
(a) First
(b) Second
(c) Third
(d) Fourth

112. Who is responsible for introducing the concept of stored program
(a) Blaise Pascal
(b) Herman Hollerith
(c) Charles Babbage
(d) John Von Nuemann

113. Which American computer company is called Big Blue?
(a) IBM
(b) Microsoft Corporation
(c) Tandy Svenson
(d) Compaq Corporation

114. A group of characters that are treated as a single entity
(a) Bit
(b) Byte
(c) Word
(d) Address

115. The computer code for the interchange of information between terminal is
(a) BCD
(b) EBCDIC

(c) ASCH
(d) Hollerith

116. Which of the following is not a Magnetic memory
(a) Core
(b) Flip-flop
(c) Disk
(d) Tape

117. One advantage of RAM is that it is
(a) Slow
(b) Bulky
(c) Volatile
(d) More power consuming

118. Which part of the system allows the user to interact with Computer?
(a) Interpreter
(b) Translator
(c) CPU
(d) Main Memory

119. A CPUs procesing power is measured in
(a) IPS
(b) CIPS
(c) Nano-seconds
(d) MIPS

Answers

1	(d)	2	(b)	3	(a)	4	(c)	5	(c)
6	(d)	7	(c)	8	(a)	9	(d)	10	(a)
11	(d)	12	(d)	13	(c)	14	(a)	15	(a)
16	(a)	17	(d)	18	(c)	19	(d)	20	(d)
21	(d)	22	(b)	23	(b)	24	(b)	25	(a)
26	(a)	27	(d)	28	(a)	29	(d)	30	(d)
31	(a)	32	(a)	33	(a)	34	(a)	35	(c)
36	(d)	37	(d)	38	(c)	39	(c)	40	(d)
41	(d)	42	(c)	43	(b)	44	(c)	45	(d)
46	(d)	47	(b)	48	(a)	49	(b)	50	(a)
51	(b)	52	(b)	53	(b)	54	(d)	55	(c)
56	(a)	57	(b)	58	(b)	59	(c)	60	(d)
61	(a)	62	(d)	63	(d)	64	(b)	65	(b)
66	(b)	67	(d)	68	(c)	69	(a)	70	(c)
71	(a)	72	(b)	73	(d)	74	(a)	75	(a)
76	(b)	77	(a)	78	(a)	79	(c)	80	(a)
81	(a)	82	(d)	83	(b)	84	(b)	85	(c)
86	(a)	87	(d)	88	(b)	89	(d)	90	(a)
91	(d)	92	(d)	93	(a)	94	(a)	95	(b)
96	(c)	97	(c)	98	(b)	99	(a)	100	(a)
101	(c)	102	(d)	103	(c)	104	(b)	105	(a)
106	(d)	107	(a)	108	(d)	109	(d)	110	(c)
111	(d)	112	(a)	113	(a)	114	(c)	115	(d)
116	(c)	117	(c)	118	(d)	119	(d)		

BOOKS & AUTHORS

1 Who among the following wrote a treatise on Medicine in ancient India?

(a) Aryabhatta (b) Charaka
(c) Nagarjuna (d) Varahmihir

2 The author of 'Hind Swaraj' was:

(a) V. D. Savarkar (b) Mahatma Gandhi
(c) B. G. Tilak (d) None of these

3 Which of the following books was banned by all Muslim countries including India?

(a) Shame (b) Freedom at midnight
(c) Satanic Verses (d) None of these

4 Daur-i-Humayun was written by:

(a) Babur (b) Gubban Begum
(c) Humayun (d) Khanzada Begum

5 The oldest Hindu epic is:

(a) Mahabhashya (b) Ramayana
(c) Mahabharata (d) Ashtadhyayi

6 Charaka Samhita is a work on:

(a) Politics (b) Economics
(c) Mathematics (d) Medicine

7 Who was the author of the book which had been banned by all Muslim Countries, including India?

(a) Salman Rushdie (b) A. Asif Ali
(c) George Orwell (d) None or these

8 Who wrote the book titled 'Runs and Ruins'?

(a) Kapil Dev (b) Sunil Gavaskar
(c) Imran Khan (d) None of these

9 Who wrote 'As you like it' ?

(a) Bernard Shaw (b) William Shakespeare
(c) Leo Tolstoy (d) Mulk Raj Anand

10 'Das Capital' is written by:

(a) Lenin (b) Karl Marx
(c) Mao-Tse-Lung (d) None of these

11 Who is the author of 'The Great Depression of 1990' ?

(a) Ravi Batra (b) R. K. Narayan
(c) M. V. Kamath (d) Khushwant Singh

12 'Ain-i-Akbari is written by:
(a) Firdausi (b) Abul Fazal
(c) Ghalib (d) None of these

13 Who wrote 'A Passage to India'?
(a) E. M. Foster (b) Minoo Masani
(c) Jawaharlal Nehru (d) None of these

14 Who is the author of the famous play 'Hall a Bal'
(a) Uma Shankar (b) Safadar Hashmi
(c) Vatsayan (d) Khushwant Singh

15 Who wrote the 'Nacked Triangle' ?
(a) Balwant Gargi (b) Amrita Pritam
(c) Khushwant Singh (d) None of these

16 Kautilya's 'Arthashastra' is a:
(a) Law Book (b) Hymns
(c) Treatise (d) A Letter

17 Who is the author of 'Swami and friends':
(a) R. K. Laxman (b) Mulk Raj Anand
(c) R. K. Narayan (d) None of these

18 'Post Office' is written by:
(a) R. K. Narayan (b) R. K. Laxman
(c) Mulk Raj Anand (d) Rabindra Nath Tagore

19 Who is the author of 'Anand Math' ?
(a) Iqbal
(b) Tara Shankar Bandhopadhyaya
(c) None or these
(d) Bankim Chandra Chatterjee

20 'Panchatantra' was written by:
(a) Bhasa (b) Vishnu Sharma
(c) Jaya Deva (d) Banbhatta

21 Who is the author of 'Nineteen Eighty Four' ?
(a) J. M. Barrie (b) George Orwell
(c) Sir Walter Scot (d) Thomas Hardy

22 The author of 'Shahnama and Akbarnama' are respectively:

(a) Firdausi and Abul Fazal
(b) Abul Fazal and Sheikh Sayed
(c) Abul Fazal and Firdausi
(d) None of these

23 'Rig Veda' chiefly contains:
(a) Early Aryan Culture
(b) Collections of hymns to God
(c) Methods of Vedic Yagnas
(d) Origin of Hindu Gods

24 The author of 'Arthashastra' is:
(a) Kalidas (b) Kautilya
(c) Bhavabhuti (d) None of these

25 The author of 'Malavikagnimitra' is:
(a) Harishena
(b) Kalidas
(c) Vatsabhatti
(d) Bhavabhuti

26 The number of Upanishads are:
(a) Eleven
(b) Twelve
(c) Fourteen
(d) Fifteen

27 The author of 'Geet Govinda' is:
(a) M. K. Gandhi
(b) Jayadeva
(c) Mulk Raj Anand
(d) Prem Chand

28 'Life Divine' is written by:
(a) Mulk Raj Anand
(b) Aurobindo Ghosh
(c) Abul Kalam Azad
(d) Jawaharlal Nehru

29 'India Wins Freedom' is the autobiography of:
(a) Jawaharlal Nehru
(b) Maulana Abul Kalam Azad
(c) M. K. Gandhi
(d) None of these

30 'Meghdoot' was written by:
(a) Bhavabhuti (b) Kalidasa
(c) Maharishi Vedvyas (d) Maharishi Valmiki

31 'Rajtarangini' was written by:
(a) Jayadeva (b) Kalhana
(c) Somadeva (d) Banabhatta

32 Who rendered the English translation of 'India Wins Freedom' ?
(a) Humayun Kabir
(b) Jawahar Lal Nehru
(c) Maulana Abul Kalam Azad
(d) None of these

33 Who is the author of 'India Divided' ?
(a) Jawaharlal Nehru (b) Maulana Abul Kalam Azad
(c) Rajendra Prasad (d) Humayun Kabir

34 The author who lives in tight security in England because Ayatullah Khomeini, the Iranian spiritual leader passed a death sentence on him is:
(a) Salman Rushdie (b) E. M. Forster
(c) K. Asaf Ali (d) None of these

35 'Mitakshara' the ancient book was written by:
(a) Rajashekhar (b) Vijneswara
(c) Somadeva (d) None of these

36 'Matta Vitarr' is written by:
(a) Harsha (b) Somadeva
(c) Manendra Vikram (d) Rajashekhar

37 The most important divinity in the 'Rig Veda' is:
(a) Agni (b) Maruti
(c) Varuna (d) Indra

38 Which of the following Acts enabled the Government of India to put a ban on 'The Satanic Verses' by Salman Rushdie?
(a) National Security Act
(b) Customs Act
(c) Immoral Trafficking Act
(d) None of these

39 Who is the author of 'A suitable boy' ?
(a) R. K. Narayan

(b) Nirad C. Chaudhary
(c) Amitava Ghosh
(d) Vikram Seth

40 Who is the author of the controversial book 'Gratha Adi Shree Guru Grantha Sahib'?
(a) Akhilesh Jaiswal
(b) Dr. Piar Singh
(c) Dr. Rita Joshi
(d) Dr. Piara Singh

Answers

1	(b)	2	(b)	3	(c)	4	(b)	5	(b)
6	(d)	7	(a)	8	(b)	9	(b)	10	(b)
11	(a)	12	(b)	13	(a)	14	(b)	15	(a)
16	(c)	17	(c)	18	(d)	19	(c)	20	(b)
21	(b)	22	(a)	23	(d)	24	(b)	25	(b)
26	(a)	27	(b)	28	(b)	29	(b)	30	(b)
31	(b)	32	(a)	33	(c)	34	(a)	35	(b)
36	(c)	37	(c)	38	(b)	39	(d)	40	(b)

FAMOUS PERSONALITIES

1 Who is known as the 'Father of Geometry' ?
(a) Keppler (b) Euclid
(c) Pythogoras (d) Newton

2 Mira Ben was a follower of:
(a) Vinoba Bhave (b) Mahatma Gandhi
(c) Pandit Nehru (d) None of these

3 Aryabhatta was India's renowned:
(a) Poet (b) Physicist
(c) Mathematician (d) Medical Practitioner

4 In which of the fields did Tenzing Norgey distinguish himself?
(a) Hockey (b) Mountaineering
(c) Boxing (d) Cycling

5 Who advocated the theory of 'laissez faire' ?
(a) Marshall (b) Adam Smith
(c) Malthus (d) None of these

6 Who among the following is known as 'Fahrer' ?
(a) Stalin (b) Bismark
(c) Lenin (d) Hitler

7 Who discovered the sea route to India?
(a) Vasco de Gama (b) Columbus
(c) Magellan (d) Hopkins

8 Who is known as the 'Iron man of India' ?
(a) Jawahar Lal Nehru (b) Bal Gangadhar Tilak
(c) Mahatma Gandhi (d) Sardar Vallabhbhai Patel

9 Otto Von Bismark is called
(a) Grand Commoner (b) Man of Blood and Iron
(c) Grand Old Man (d) Man of Destiny

10 'The Rama Krishna Mission' was started by:
(a) Swami Vivekanand
(b) Ramakrishna Paramhansa
(c) Swami Dayanand Saraswati
(d) None or these

11 Who among the following is not associated with 'Swaraj Party' ?
(a) C. R. Dass (b) M. L. Kelkar

(c) Motilal Nehru (d) Mahatma Gandhi

12 Marie Montessori's name is associated with:
(a) Christian Mission (b) Child Education
(c) Women's rights (d) Mission Hospitals

13 Who is known as 'Deshbandhu' ?
(a) Chandra Shekhar (b) C. R. Das
(c) A. O. Hume (d) Annie Basent

14 Marshall Tito was:
(a) President of Egypt (b) A Hero of the World War II
(c) President of Yugoslavia (d) None of these

15 Where was Albert Einstein born?
(a) UK (b) Germany
(c) USA (d) Albania

16 Kalidas was:
(a) A poet during Gupta period
(b) A dramatist during Harshavardhana's reign
(c) An astronomer during the Gupta period
(d) None of these

17 Gopal Krishna Gokhale's name is associated with:
(a) Hindu Mahasabha
(b) Servants Society of India
(c) Brahmo Samaj
(d) Shiv Sena

18 Who was the first lady Prime Minister of the world?
(a) Smt. Sirimavo Bhandarnaike
(b) Smt. Indira Gandhi
(c) Mrs. Magaret Thatcher
(d) Mrs. Golda Meir

19 Who was the first woman president of the Indian National Congress?
(a) Vijaylaxmi Pandit (b) Sarojini Naidu
(c) Annie Besant (d) None of these

20 The first Navigator to sail around the world was:
(a) Marco Polo (b) Amundsen
(c) Columbus (d) Magellan

21 Who among the following is known as 'Kipper' ?
(a) Napolean Bonaparte

(b) Field Marshall K. M. Kariappa
(c) Gen. Erwin Rommel
(d) Younger Ritt

22 John Maynard Keynes was:
(a) Poet (b) Scintist
(c) Mathematician (d) Economist

23 Who among the following was associated with the freedom struggle of Tanzania?
(a) Patrice Lumumba (b) Kemal Ataturk
(c) Kenneth Kaunda (d) Dr. Julius Nyerere

24 Vasco da Gama was a:
(a) Australian Navigator (b) French Navigator
(c) Portuguese Explorer (d) British Explorer

25 Who was the first woman to reach the North Pole?
(a) Mrs. Fran Phipps
(b) Ms. Valentina Tershkora
(c) Mrs. Karoline Mikkelson
(d) None of these

26 Fa Hien was a:
(a) Chinese Travellor (b) Japanese Navigator
(c) Portuguese Sailor (d) British Explorer

27 Who is known as "Little Corporal'
(a) Adolf Hitler (b) William E. Gladstone
(c) Napolean Bonaparte (d) None of these

28 Valentina Tereshkova was the first woman to:
(a) Cross the English Channel
(b) Reach North Pole
(c) Reach South Pole
(d) None of these

29 Who was the first Indian woman to scale Mt. Everest?
(a) Bachendri Pal (b) Ang Dorjee
(c) Phu Dorjee (d) None of these

30 Dhanvantri's name is associated with:
(a) Indian Medicine (b) Sanskrit Grammar
(c) Classical Music (d) Sanskrit Poetry

31 Leonardo da Vinci who is famous for his masterpiece painting 'Mona

Lisa' was a/an:
(a) French Artist (b) German Painter
(c) Italian Artist (d) None of these

32 Sridath Rampal's name is associated with:
(a) UNO (b) NAM
(c) SAARC (d) Commonwealth

33 Mother Teresa was born in:
(a) Switzerland (b) Germany
(c) India (d) Albania

34 Mrs. Vijaylakshmi Pandit was the first woman to become:
(a) Chief Minister of a State
(b) Member of Lok Sabha
(c) Member of the Rajya Sabha
(d) Minister of State

35 Who was the first human space travellor?
(a) Edwin Aldrin (USA) (b) Yuri Gagarin (Russia)
(c) Frank Boreman (USA) (d) Gherman S. Titor (Russia)

36 Martin Luther King was a:
(a) Social Reformer
(b) Secretory General of UNO
(c) Black US Civil Rights Leader
(d) None of these

37 Who pioneered the modern Nursing Home?
(a) Florence Nightingale (b) Greta Garbo
(c) Mother Teresa (d) None of these

38 Which of the following is correct?
(a) Socrates was disciple of Plato
(b) Plato was disciple of Socrates
(c) Plato was disciple of Aristotle
(d) Socrates and Plato were disciples of Aristotle

39 The first woman film star nominated or elected to the Rajya Sabha:
(a) Vajyanthimala (b) Jayalalitha
(c) Nargis Dutt (d) None of these

40 Who among the following is the inventor of a system of writing and printing for the blind?
(a) Robert Wilhelm Bunsen

(b) Braille Louis
(c) Sir Humphrey Davy
(d) Christian Haygens

Answers

1	(c)	2	(a)	3	(c)	4	(b)	5	(b)
6	(d)	7	(a)	8	(d)	9	(b)	10	(a)
11	(a)	12	(b)	13	(b)	14	(c)	15	(b)
16	(a)	17	(b)	18	(a)	19	(c)	20	(d)
21	(b)	22	(d)	23	(d)	24	(c)	25	(c)
26	(a)	27	(c)	28	(d)	29	(a)	30	(d)
31	(c)	32	(b)	33	(d)	34	(d)	35	(b)
36	(c)	37	(a)	38	(b)	39	(c)	40	(b)

SPORTS

1 Who started the ancient Olympic Games?
(a) The Romans (b) The Egyptians
(c) The Greeks (d) None of these

2 Which is India's Largest Indoor Stadium?
(a) Netaji Stadium, Kolkata
(b) Indira Gandhi Indoor Stadium, New Delhi
(c) Bharti Stadium, Cuttack
(d) None of these

3 Which is India's Largest Stadium?
(a) National Stadium, Delhi
(b) Yuba Bharati Stadium, New Delhi
(c) Yadvindra Stadium, Patiala
(d) Vallabh Bhai Patel Stadium, Mumbai

4 Who is said to be the father of modern Olympics?
(a) Robert - Dover (b) Theodusius I
(c) Pierre de Coubertin (d) Enest Curtis

5 In which year was the International Olympic Committee (IOC) fromed?
(a) 1845 (b) 1894
(c) 1875 (d) 1895

6 The Headquarters of the IOC is located in:
(a) Olympia (b) Paris
(c) Lausanne (d) Athens

7 The first recorded ancient Olympics was held in:
(a) 700 BC (b) 310 BC
(c) 776 BC (d) 450 BC

8 Modern Olympics was revived by:
(a) A Dutch nobleman (b) A French nobleman
(c) A Greek nobleman (d) A German nobleman

9 The symbol of the Summer Olympic Games comprises of:
(a) Five rings of the same colour
(b) Five rings of different colours
(c) Four blue rings
(d) Four rings of different colours

10 Where was the first Olympic Games held?
(a) Olypia (b) Seoul
(c) Athens (d) Los Angeles

11 The Summer Olympic Games are normally held at intervals of:
(a) 3 Yrs. (b) 4 Yrs.
(c) 3 Yrs. (d) 5 Yrs.

12 The Winter Olympic Games came into being in the year:
(a) 1908 (b) 1916
(c) 1912 (d) 1924

13 Which Olympic Games had to be cancelled due to World War I?
(a) 1908 (b) 1912
(c) 1916 (d) None of these

14 Which country led a boycott of the 1980 Olympic Games held in Moscow?
(a) Great Britain (b) United States
(c) China (d) South Korea

15 When did the first Commonwealth Games take place:
(a) 1948 (b) 1934
(c) 1930 (d) 1945

16 In which year were the 15th Commonwealth Games held?
(a) 1982 (b) 1990
(c) 1984 (d) 1988

17 The Commonwealth Games normally take place at an interval of:
(a) 3 Yrs. (b) 4 Yrs.
(c) 5 Yrs. (d) None of these

18 The Commonwealth Games had to be cancelled during:
(a) 1942 (b) 1942 & 1946
(c) 1946 (d) 1948

19 In which year were the first Asian Games held?
(a) 1947 (b) 1955
(c) 1951 (d) 1958

20 Which among the following countries hosted the first Asian Games?
(a) India (b) China
(c) Indonesia (d) Former USSR

21 Which country hosted the XI the Asiad?

(a) Former W. Germany (b) S. Korea
(c) China (d) USSR

22 How many medals did P.T. Usha win individually in the X Asiad?
(a) 3 (b) 4
(c) 2 (d) 5

23 How many medals did P.T. Usha win in the Asiad X ?
(a) 3 (b) 4
(c) 2 (d) 5

24 Which Game is associated with the Durand Cup?
(a) Hockey (b) Football
(c) Badminton (d) Tennis

25 Which of the following cup is associated with badminton?
(a) William Todd Memorial Trophy
(b) Uber Cup
(c) Holkar Trophy
(d) None of these

26 Ranji Trophy and Aga Khan Cup are associated with:
(a) Cricket & Hockey
(b) Badminton & Hockey
(c) Cricket & Football
(d) Cricket & Volleyball

27 Which of the Trophies below is not associated with cricket:
(a) Duleep Trophy
(b) Champions Trophy
(c) Charminar Challange Cup
(d) Rohinton Trophy

28 Brooklyn (USA) is associated with:
(a) Golf (b) Baseball
(c) Snooker (d) Tennis

29 With which game is Brook land (England) associated?
(a) Hockey (b) Football
(c) Tennis (d) Golf

30 Which of the following games are associated with Davis Cup?
(a) Volleyball (b) Tennis
(c) Badminton (d) Handball

31 The Dronacharya Award is associated with:

(a) Hockey captains for the World Cup
(b) Sports Coaches
(c) Boxing Championship
(d) None of these

32 The Dronacharya Award for Sports Coaches was instituted in:
(a) 1984 (b) 1987
(c) 1985 (d) 1988

33 Merdeka Cup is associated with:
(a) Badminton (b) Hockey
(c) Volleyball (d) Football

34 Reliance Cup is associated with:
(a) Hockey (b) Cricket
(c) Tennis (d) Football

35 In Cricket Long Top is:
(a) The position before the bowler
(b) The position behind the batsman
(c) The position on the left side of the batsman
(d) None of these

36 Among the following term 'pick out the one' associated with Hockey:
(a) Short Corner (b) Bully
(c) Dribble (d) Hat Trick

37 Grand Prix is associated with:
(a) Lawn Tennis (b) Volleyball
(c) Boxing (d) Golf

38 Wimbledon is associated with which of the Games?
(a) Golf (b) Cricket
(c) Badminton (d) None of these

39 The term 'Dribbling' is not associated with:
(a) Hockey (b) Basketball
(c) Baseball (d) Football

40 The term 'smash' in sports is associated with:
(a) Lawn Tennis (b) Badminton
(c) Hockey (d) None of these

41 The term 'boggy' is associated with:
(a) Tennis (b) Baseball
(c) Chess (d) Golf

42 Pivot is associated with which of the following games?
(a) Hockey (b) Golf
(c) Tennis (d) Basketball

43 The term 'deuce' is common in which of the following two games?
(a) Basketball & Badminton
(b) Badminton & Tennis
(c) Volleyball & Tennis
(d) None of these

44 The term 'L.B.W.' is associated with:
(a) Hockey (b) Chess
(c) Football (d) Cricket

45 How many players are there in a football team?
(a) 10 (b) 7
(c) 6 (d) 11

46 How many players are there on each side in a Women's Basketball Game?
(a) 5 (b) 7
(c) 6 (d) 10

47 Dhyan Chand's name is associated with which game?
(a) Football (b) Badminton
(c) Hockey (d) Tennis

48 'Play the game in the spirit of game', was said by:
(a) G. S. Sondhi (b) Pt. Nehru
(c) Coubertin (d) None of these

49 Which sport returned to Olympics in 1988 after 64 years?
(a) Indo (b) Croquet
(c) Tennis (d) Canoeing

50 Which of the sports was introduced in the 1988 Seoul Olympic Games?
(a) Tennis (b) Table Tennis
(c) Badminton (d) Rowing

Answers

1	(c)	2	(b)	3	(b)	4	(c)	5	(b)
6	(c)	7	(c)	8	(b)	9	(b)	10	(c)
11	(b)	12	(d)	13	(c)	14	(b)	15	(c)
16	(b)	17	(b)	18	(b)	19	(c)	20	(a)
21	(c)	22	(a)	23	(b)	24	(b)	25	(b)
26	(a)	27	(b)	28	(b)	29	(b)	30	(b)
31	(b)	32	(c)	33	(d)	34	(b)	35	(b)
36	(b)	37	(a)	38	(c)	39	(c)	40	(b)
41	(d)	42	(d)	43	(b)	44	(d)	45	(d)
46	(c)	47	(c)	48	(b)	49	(c)	50	(b)

ART & ARCHITECTURE

1 Name the Greek poet who is credited with drawing up the list of the Seven wonders of the Ancient World.
(a) Antipater of Sidon
(b) G. B. Shaw
(c) Henry Fielding
(d) Louis Fischer

2 What is the name given to the Japanese art of cultivating dwarf trees?
(a) Bosani
(b) Bosnia
(c) Bonsai
(d) Bensa

3 Name of the Spanish sculptor and painter who is known as the Father of the Modern Art.
(a) Pablo Picasso
(b) Wells
(c) Monison
(d) Bassie

4 What architectural structures were considered by ancient Egyptians as 'a staircase to heaven being laid out for the king'?
(a) Tombs
(b) The Palaces
(c) The Pyramids
(d) None of these

5 Name three art styles that were used by the ancient Greeks for building their columns.
(a) Doric
(b) Iconic
(c) Corinthian
(d) All of these

6 What is the name of the famous wax museum at London?
(a) Wax
(b) London Museum
(c) Madane Museum
(d) Madame Tussaud's

7 What is the art, of trimming trees into ornamental shapes and objects known as?
(a) Topology
(b) Topograph
(c) Topiary
(d) Topilogy

8 What name is given to the Japanese art of folding paper into various decorative forms?
(a) Oriamy
(b) Origamy
(c) Orian
(d) Oriana

9 Name the place where the world's oldest Castle is situated?
(a) Yemen
(b) Tokyo
(c) Beijing
(d) Seol

10 By what other name was the temple of Artemis at Ephesus known?
(a) Ephesus Temple
(b) Temple Mayane
(c) Temple of Diana
(d) The Temple of Christ

11 What is the name given to the art of drawing or printing on stone?
(a) Cratography
(b) Cratology
(c) Lithography
(d) Lithology

12 Of the seven wonders of the Ancient world one is still standing. What is its name?
(a) Pyramids of Giza
(b) Pyramids of Gaza
(c) Pyramids of Ghana
(d) None of these

13 To which Pharaoh, the largest of the three Giza pyramids belong?
(a) King Kaif
(b) King Khufu
(c) King Lost

(d) King Adward

14 The helicopter was designed by a famous Italian artist, renowned sculptor and inventor. Name him.
(a) Leonardo
(b) Vinci
(c) Leonardo de Vinci
(d) Edgar

15 What is 'Choreography' ?
(a) Art of Dance
(b) Dancing Movements
(c) Art of Painting
(d) Art of Singing

16 Who is a 'Choreographer' ?
(a) Composer of Dance
(b) Composer of Song
(c) Composer of Music
(d) Composer of Lyric

17 By whom was the famous sculpture Apollo and Daphne created?
(a) G. L. Bernini
(b) A. Bernini
(c) Virginia Woolf
(d) None of these

18 Name one of the Seven wonders of the Ancient world that was constructed at the ancient city of Halicarnassus in Asia Minor.
(a) The Tomb of Mausolus
(b) The Tomb of Musa
(c) The Tomb of Aries
(d) None of these

19 Name of the eminent German family that produced musicians over Seven generations.
(a) Von Goethe
(b) Bach
(c) Haksar
(d) Carey

20 Which famous German composer continued writing musical pieces even after he turned deaf?
(a) L. V. Beethoven

(b) Von Goethe
(c) Haksar
(d) Carey

21 Name the famous American Comedian who produced, directed, composed music and acted in his films?
(a) D. Chaplin
(b) Charlie Chaplin
(c) S. Harry
(d) Johny

22 Name the king who built the Hanging Gardens of Babylon.
(a) Nebuchadnezzar II
(b) Bebuchadnezzar I
(c) Nebuchadnezzar III
(d) Bebuchadnezzar IV

23 Name the Greek Sculptor who designed the statue of Zesus at Olympia.
(a) Conrad
(b) Lud lumb
(c) Austen
(d) Phidias

24 Name the Venetian painter of Paradise, the largest of oil paintings on Canvas?
(a) Vannegut
(b) Tintoretto
(c) Porter
(d) Lawrence

25 What is the name of the style of painting for which Pablo Picasso became famous?
(a) Cubusm
(b) Cubism
(c) Kate
(d) Krote

26 What is the name of the giant statue dedicated to the Greek Sun God Helios and is one of the Seven wonders of the Ancient World?
(a) The Great Helios
(b) The Great Greek
(c) The Colossus

(d) Colossus of Rhodes

27 Which Russian musician composed the ballet The Firebird in 1910?
(a) Igor Stavinsky
(b) Ian Starvonsky
(c) Solzhenitsyn
(d) Ian Clovesky

28 Name the city in which Colosseum is situated.
(a) Paris
(b) Washington
(c) Rome
(d) Geneva

29 Which dog is generally adopted by Cartoonists to symbolise the British character?
(a) Tha Catdog
(b) The Reddog
(c) The Bulldog
(d) Alsisiandog

30 Name the systematic study of the varying forms of pictorial symbols.
(a) Ionography
(b) Icography
(c) Iconography
(d) Ideography

31 Name the country where the Leaning Tower of Pisa is situated?
(a) France
(b) Germany
(c) Russia
(d) Italy

32 What is the present name of the building in U.S.A. which was earlier called the 'Executive Mansion'?
(a) President Mansion
(b) Peace House
(c) Lotus House
(d) The White House

33 Name the art and literary movement wherein forms and imagery give full play to the imagination and the subconscious?
(a) Surelism
(b) Sereliam

(c) Surrealism
(d) Sorolism

34 Name the French Sculptor who created 'The Thinker'.
(a) Paul Satre
(b) Auguste Rodin
(c) Both 'a' and 'b'
(d) None of these

35 Name the European city where the Elysee Palace is situated.
(a) London
(b) Rome
(c) Paris
(d) Vatican City

36 Name the Florentine painter who created the famous 'The creation of Adam'.
(a) Michelangelo
(b) Scott
(c) Fragson
(d) Burroughs

37 Name the largest airport of the world.
(a) Abdul-Aziz International Airport, Jeddah
(b) Indira Gandhi International Airport, New Delhi
(c) Chicago International Airport
(d) New York International Airport

38 What is the name of the tallest statue in the world?
(a) Motherland
(b) Fatherland
(c) Statue of Lenin
(d) Statue of Marx

39 Where in the world is the Great Sphinx situated?
(a) Gaza
(b) Giza
(c) Zairo
(d) None of these

40 What are Cleopatra's Needles?
(a) Large Block of Stone
(b) Single Block of Stone
(c) Both 'a' and 'b'

(d) None of these

41 Name the largest residential Palace in the world.
(a) White House
(b) Buckingham Palace
(c) Vatican Palace
(d) Moscow House

42 In America which building is known as the 'Pentagon'?
(a) Headquarters of the Department of Defence of USA
(b) Headquarters of the Department of Home of USA
(c) Headquarters of CIA
(d) Headquarters of UNO

43 Name the European city where Eiffel Tower is located.
(a) Geneva
(b) Rome
(c) Paris
(d) London

44 Which is the heaviest bell in the world?
(a) Tsar Kolokol
(b) Tsar Kaki
(c) Heavy Bell
(d) None of these

45 Where is the 'Sydney Opera House' located.
(a) Perth
(b) Sydney
(c) Brisbane
(d) Canberra

46 Name the place where 'Christ The Redeemer' statue is situated.
(a) Rio de Janeiro
(b) Geneva
(c) Seoul
(d) Madrid

47 Where is the 'Great Wall' located?
(a) Northern China
(b) Southern China
(c) North-West China
(d) South-West China

48 Where is Parthenon Temple situated?
(a) Los Angeles
(b) Athens
(c) Atlanta
(d) Washington

49 Where is The Taj Mahal situated?
(a) Delhi
(b) Sikandra
(c) Agra
(d) Aurangabad

50 Name the painter of the 'The Creation of Man'
(a) Michelangelo
(b) Russell
(c) Monison
(d) Crosette

51 Who painted the master piece 'A Midnight Modern Civilisation'?
(a) Michelangelo
(b) Hogarth
(c) Morrison
(d) Crosette

52 Who created the masterpiece 'The birth of Venus'
(a) Botticeli
(b) Hogarth
(c) Michelangelo
(d) Crosette

53 Who is the painter of 'The blue boy'?
(a) Botticeli
(b) Hogarth
(c) Gains Borrough
(d) Crosette

54 By whom was the master piece 'View of Toledo' created?
(a) El Greco
(b) Botticeli
(c) Hogarth
(d) Michelangelo

55 Who is the painter of 'The Cry' ?
(a) Vangogh

(b) Botticeli
(c) El Greco
(d) Hogarth

56 Name the painter of 'The School of Athens'.
(a) Vangogh
(b) Raphael
(c) El Greco
(d) Botticeli

57 By whom was 'Shakuntala' created? (Name the painter)
(a) Raja Ravi Verma
(b) Jatin Das
(c) C. Poddar
(d) M. F. Hussain

58 Name the painter of 'The Stalmeesters".
(a) Raphael
(b) El Greco
(c) Rembrant
(d) Hogarth

59 Where is the Lalit Kala Academy situated?
(a) Mumbai
(b) Delhi
(c) Chennai
(d) Kolkata

60 Name the painter of 'The Death of Marat'.
(a) David
(b) Monet
(c) Demuth
(d) Raphael

61 Name the painter of 'Water Lilies'.
(a) Hogarth
(b) Monet
(c) Botticelli
(d) None of these

62 Name the painter of 'Afternoon on the grand Jatte'.
(a) Seurat
(b) Monet
(c) Raphael
(d) None of these

Answers

1	(b)	2	(d)	3	(a)	4	(b)	5	(a)
6	(a)	7	(d)	8	(a)	9	(b)	10	(c)
11	(d)	12	(a)	13	(c)	14	(c)	15	(a)
16	(b)	17	(c)	18	(a)	19	(b)	20	(c)
21	(a)	22	(b)	23	(a)	24	(b)	25	(b)
26	(c)	27	(a)	28	(a)	29	(b)	30	(a)
31	(b)	32	(c)	33	(a)	34	(b)	35	(c)
36	(a)	37	(b)	38	(a)	39	(b)	40	(a)
41	(b)	42	(c)	43	(a)	44	(b)	45	(a)
46	(b)	47	(c)	48	(b)	49	(b)	50	(c)
51	(b)	52	(d)	53	(a)	54	(b)	55	(d)
56	(b)	57	(c)	58	(a)	59	(b)	60	(c)
61	(a)	62	(b)						